Lalique
for
Collectors

Lalique
for
Collectors

❧❧

Katharine Morrison McClinton

CHARLES SCRIBNER'S SONS / NEW YORK

Copyright © 1975 Katharine M. McClinton

Library of Congress Cataloging in Publication Data

McClinton, Katharine Morrison.
    Lalique for collectors.

    Bibliography: p.
    Includes index.
    1. Lalique, René, 1860-   2. Glassware, French.
3. Decoration and ornament—Art nouveau.   4. Art deco.
I. Title.
NK5198.L44.M32   748.2'9'24   74-14015
ISBN 0-684-15863-9

1 3 5 7 9 11 13 15 17 19 **C/MD** 20 18 16 14 12 10 8 6 4 2

Printed in the United States of America

*For Erma
with affection and appreciation*

ACKNOWLEDGEMENTS

My appreciation for valuable assistance in the gathering of material for this book goes to the following:

Robert Sistrunk, Antaeus Gallery Inc.
Richard Peters and Sheldon Barr, Sybarites Gallery Inc.
John Jesse, London, England
Lillian and Paul Nassau
Minna Rosenblatt
Barry Friedman
Felix Marcilhac, Paris, France
Martin Cohen
Dennis R. Anderson, Curator of Decorative Arts,
    Chrysler Museum at Norfolk, Virginia
Christian Rohlfing, Administrative Director,
    Cooper-Hewitt Museum of Decorative Arts and Design

I also owe a special thank you to my editor, Elinor Parker, for her careful reading and editing of the manuscript.

Contents

Introduction

THE ART OF RENE LALIQUE IS UNIQUE IN THAT IT COVERED two periods of decorative styles—Art Nouveau and Art Deco. Lalique's jewelry was the finest goldsmith's work produced in Art Nouveau style. He was not a follower but an innovator and his jewelry produced in the 1890s revolutionized the design and materials of the goldsmith's art. Lalique was more concerned with the decorative element and craftsmanship than he was with materials. His pieces of jewelry became valuable and highly stylized small works of art. Instead of precious expensive stones he used irregular-shaped baroque pearls, semi-precious stones, enamel, and translucent horn. He made brooches, combs, pendants, and other pieces of jewelry in his own imaginative non-traditional forms. In his jewelry Lalique combined all the forms and materials of plastic art.

After the Universal Exhibition of 1900 Lalique found himself deluged with more jewelry commissions than he could fill. Also there were many imitators who debased his style. Although Lalique continued to produce jewelry for a number of years more he lost his incentive and his interest gradually turned to glass. Lalique had already studied and experimented with glass. He had included small beads of glass and medallions and plaques of colored *pâte-de-verre* in his articles of gold and enamelled jewelry and he had made cups and small flacons of glass. Soon after 1900 his interest centered on glass-making; he began specializing in the production of small flacons and *services de table*. In 1898 Lalique exhibited a glass and silver vase, and in the 1902 Salon he showed two *coupes*.

In about 1902 Lalique acquired a small glassworks at Clairfontaine in the forest near Rambouillet where he set up a small kiln and employed four workers. Here Lalique made experimental statuettes, unique *cire perdue* vases, and glass panels which he mounted in doors and chandeliers. About this time Lalique designed and built his sumptuous premises at 40, cours de la Reine in Paris where he installed his workshop and all his services. The doors of the house had panels of *pâte-de-verre* and he also created the furniture and interior decorations and architectural embellishments. In 1905 a shop for the sale of his artifacts was opened at Place Vendôme No. 24.

In 1907-1908 when François Coty invited Lalique to design bottles for his perfumes Lalique accepted the commission with enthusiasm and this collaboration was successful from the start. Later Lalique designed bottles for other perfume manufacturers. The bottles were made by Legras & Cie. de St. Denis, a glass manufacturer with a factory on the Seine.

In 1909 Lalique opened his own glassworks at Combs called "Verrerie de Combs-la-Ville." Here Lalique manufactured his glass vases, lamps, statuettes, and various small accessories of glass executed in molds with applied foliage, animals, and insects. The pieces were also often ornamented with engraving and enamel. These pieces were exhibited in 1912 for the first time and this date also marks the end of Lalique's production of metal jewelry.

Between 1918 and 1922 Lalique constructed a large glassworks at Wingen sur Moder in the Bas-Rhin called "Verrerie d'Alsace René Lalique & Cie."

Here Lalique produced articles of molded glass on a large commercial scale with hundreds of reproductions of each article. With his cast glass with molded ornament (*"verre moulé décoré en creux"*) Lalique again became an innovator. Although Lalique's importance as a glassmaker came late in the period, the designs of his major production of glass are easily traced to Art Nouveau. Yet like the majority of the artists at this time Lalique reacted against Art Nouveau which had now become cheapened by commercialism. In his search for a new decorative idiom Lalique turned to the stylized forms of Art Deco for much of his glass. Here Lalique again showed his originality, for although the majority of the glassworkers were creating glass with designs of many colors Lalique's glass was monotone. He was interested in the natural qualities of the glass and the form of the articles as much as he was in the ornamentation.

In Lalique's career as a *verrerier* his aims were strictly commercial and he sought to sell as many reproductions of his creations as possible. The glass was mass-produced and hundreds of copies were made of each piece, but a high quality of design and originality was always present. Although the concept of the original model was by Lalique—some later by his grand-daughter—Lalique did not play any active part in the making of the glass except supervising the manufacture. Lalique had a thoroughly modern attitude toward his glass. He accepted mechanical methods of production which allowed him to sell at prices within the reach of many. His color was monotone and the shapes were simple and rational. The decoration consisted of motifs from nature, female figures, and children. His dinner services and perfume flasks made Lalique glass known to the general public and his lighting fixtures and features such as portals and fountains of Lalique design were architecturally useable. Also, since Lalique glass was unlike any glass made previously, its originality and decorative qualities made it in constant demand in France, and in England as well.

By 1925 Lalique had become the most important manufacturer of fine mass-produced glass in France and at the Exposition Internationale des Arts Décoratifs et Industriels Modernes held in Paris in that year Lalique was commissioned to design the fountains and glass portal of the exposition. Examples of Lalique glass were also to be found in the various French pavilions of the exposition. The most important Lalique exhibit apart from the fountains and screens was the dining room in Le Pavillon de la Manufacture Nationale de Sèvres with its beams of molded glass designed by Lalique and lighted from concealed panels. On the massive glass table was a setting of Sèvres porcelain and wine glasses and candlesticks of molded and engraved Lalique glass.

Architectural glass was one of Lalique's most important contributions. Lalique's churches and shrines are outstanding works of modern ecclesiastic art. He designed complete altars with crucifixes, candlesticks, and reredos of molded glass. The glass panels, windows back of the altar, and the glass altar rail in the Chapelle de la Vierge Fidèle all have the Madonna lily as a motif. Lalique also designed many figurines of the Virgin and Saints.

When the French Line ship "Normandie" was launched in 1932 she carried important examples of Lalique glass. The main dining salon, 305 feet in length, 46 feet in width, and 25 feet in height, had walls constructed of thirty-eight glass panels, and the room was lighted by two gigantic chandeliers and twelve decorative standard lights of Lalique glass.

Through the offices of Breves Galleries, London, a great deal of Lalique glass paneling and lighting fixtures was used in important decorating projects in England in the 1930s. Lalique maintained his important position during the Depresssion period and each year his repertory of stock designs was increased. He managed to keep up with the times since his style evolution followed the changes that affected design generally. However, in 1937 Lalique closed the factory at Combs-la-Ville and between 1939 and 1946 all production of Lalique glass was discontinued. The factory was partially destroyed in the war and the craftsmen scattered, and in 1945 Lalique died. Although the firm continues today the majority of the most beautiful and artistic pieces have been discontinued. In many cases the original molds were destroyed and other pieces have been found too expensive for reproduction today. This has opened the field of Lalique glass to the antiques collector. Today collecting Lalique glass has become such an active pursuit that prices have risen and Lalique glass has become an important and expensive field for only the advanced collector.

The following quotation from *The Architectural Review*, February, 1928, which was reprinted in the Breves Galleries catalogue of "Lalique Lights and Decorations" is an indication of the esteem and popularity of Lalique at the height of his career. He is described as "Artist Master Craftsman"—at once an honorable and perfect description of René Lalique.

> For he is an artist in an artist's sense of the word; his knowledge is so secure that he is able to bring elimination to a fine point; each line of his design is essential, he never strikes a false note.
>
> Lalique served a long apprenticeship; he originally began life as a goldsmith and jeweller. This helps to explain the beautiful delicacy of his work and the extraordinary detail which he introduces into his glass work, detail which, though it delights the eye, never obscures the meaning and pleasure of the whole design.
>
> The simplest forms of Nature delight him most, and in his translation of them one sees one of the most attractive facets of his genius. . . .
>
> With his human figures the chief thought which comes to one's mind is their rhythm. One knows, of course, that they are static, but the feeling of movement is so brilliantly expressed that one subconsciously carries on the movement and the figures live again.
>
> When he uses colour (always with great restraint) it is always to enhance the meaning; be it a hunting scene with archers he chooses dark ruby, be it mermaids and fishes he takes the pearly blue light over the sea at dawn.
>
> One may sum up his genius aptly in the words of Paul Fallot: 'His palette is sumptuous, but always temperate, he loves delicate harmonies, tone on tone, and in his invention of forms his fantasies obey the order of logic.'

A later estimate is not so generous. It speaks of the "increasing over-elaboration of Lalique's designs." Also a gross abuse of the decorative resources of acid-engraved and sandblasted glass and of sentimentality is present in some of Lalique's designs. Lalique had found a popular repertory of design motifs and these were repeated again and again from important vases to paperweights and tiny ashtrays, and this commercialism sometimes interferes with our final estimate of his present place in the glass world.

Lalique glass contains over 24 percent lead oxide and therefore it is properly termed "lead crystal." Crystal is composed, fused, and treated in the same way as ordinary glass with the fundamental difference that it contains at least 24 percent lead oxide; glass does not. Crystal when cold will catch the light and reflect it with an unmistakable metallic sheen and brilliance. Ordinary glass with no lead has no sparkle. Lead crystal also has a lasting musical tone when tapped with the finger, while glass has a dull tone. Crystal is also heavier and softer than ordinary glass which makes it easier to cut and engrave. Lalique is especially famous for his soft satin-finish lead crystal which has an unmistakable personal character of its own.

Lalique understood the glass materials and recognized their possibilities. His glass was produced in powdered form and then cast in hot metal molds. The work of Lalique depends in most cases upon shaping by blowing or pressing in a mold and therefore does not give the impression of blown glass. (Blown wares were almost always confined to stemware and large vases, however even in these instances the stem and foot of the glass and the neck of the vase were molded.)

The light passing through the glass reflects the opal-blue tints and dramatizes the designs molded on the outside. The color of Lalique glass was obtained by metal oxides added to the glass batch; and I am indebted to the collector Robert Sistrunk for the following list of metal oxides used by Lalique to produce the colors of his glass.

Gold oxide produced fiery and blue opalescents and ruby reds.
Silver produced greens.
Platinum was used for tones of gray.
Tin gave cloudy opalescent "clam broth" effects.

Black oxide of manganese produced amethysts, purples, and black. Cobalt produced blues.

Of course the color varies according to the proportions used and the basic composition of the glass batch and to the degree of heat and the length of cooking time after the addition of the coloring agent. The color of some blown vases is altered by interior casing. When enameling was desired the powdered materials were mixed with oil thus forming paint. The decorator painted the desired design on the glass with a brush and the piece was then fired in a small furnace in order to bring about the proper fusion in the enamels and their union with the glass. Parts of the molded designs were treated with acids to produce a frosted or satin effect in contrast to the bright glistening polished effects. Iridescent effects were produced on the surface of the glass by subjecting it to gaseous fumes in a muffle furnace.

Some few pieces of Lalique glass were made by the *cire perdue* or lost wax method. These designs were first modeled in wax, then covered with a ceramic paste. After the paste hardened the paste-covered model was heated to melt out the wax model. This left a hollow ceramic mold. Into this mold the molten glass was poured. When the glass had hardened the mold was broken away leaving a perfect reproduction of the wax model in glass. This method produced a unique piece.

Although some of the original Lalique designs are still in production the marks on them have been changed and no longer bear the initial "R." Collecting interest is usually confined to the years before René Lalique's death in 1945. One way of judging the age of the glass is to look for signs of wear on the embossed surfaces.

The "Catalogue des Verreries de René Lalique" 1932 is a valuable source of information. I have given the Catalogue numbers of the articles since many pieces are marked with numbers in addition to the Lalique signature. In most cases these numbers refer to the 1932 Catalogue. However this does not mean that the piece was made at that date; in fact it indicates that it was made before 1932. The number of examples of each piece is also not exact because the Catalogue only indicates how many pieces were available, but it also is an indication of how many were actually made—whether in the hundreds or the thousands. If few pieces of a particular vase or object are listed in the Catalogue, as in the case of the vase "Méduse", it may indicate an early design which is sold out. I have given the French names of the articles since they are the key to the design but they also add romance and foreign flavor to the collecting.

Jewelry and Goldsmith Work

RENE JULES LALIQUE WAS BORN JUNE 4, 1860, AT HAY, Marne. He studied drawing at Turgot College and continued his studies at the Ecole des Arts Décoratifs in Paris during an apprenticeship to the important Paris jeweler M. Louis Aucoc. From 1878 to 1880 Lalique studied in England. When he returned to France he worked as a freelance designer for various Paris jewelers including Aucoc, Jaca, Cartier, Renn, Gariod, Hamelin, and Destape. In addition to jewelry, in the early years of his career he drew designs for fans, wallpapers, and textiles. For a short time Lalique collaborated with Charles Arfidson to furnish drawings of jewelry for the publication *Le Bijou*. In his spare time Lalique studied sculpture with the artist Lequien who was the son of his old teacher at Turgot College.

In 1883 Lalique entered a partnership with Varenne (Lalique et Varenne) which lasted two years. During this time Lalique designed many original and amusing trinkets including a balloon, a mill and a jumping jack. Lalique later took over the shop of Jules Destape where he continued to execute orders for the more important jewelers of Paris. In 1885 Lalique set up his own atelier and for the first time exhibited jewels of his own design and workmanship at the Exposition Universelle of 1889 in Paris.

In 1890 Lalique moved his atelier to larger quarters at 20, rue Thérèse, at the corner of the avenue de l'Opéra. Here he installed a complete glass workshop. He also collaborated with two sculptors and experimented in several other mediums including enameling, employing these various plastic arts in the jewelry and other artifacts which he exhibited each year in the salons.

As early as 1887 Lalique was making coffres, cups, swords, and vases. There were small flacons entwined with serpents, and a serpent's head as the stopper. Other flacons were studded with jewels. There were complete sets of *orfèvrerie de toilette* including mirrors, brushes, boxes for powder and soap, and bottles for toilet water and perfume. These articles continued to be made later when Lalique turned to commercial glassmaking. At an early date Lalique also considered making *orfèvrerie de table* including serving dishes and *couverts* of flat silver. However his jewelry was in such demand that he had no time for additional enterprises, also such articles necessitated equipping a special workshop.

In 1893 Lalique was given a prize of 500 francs for a chalice ornamented with his thistle motif. There are a group of these cups or chalices with rich ornamentation of metal, ivory, enamel, semi-precious stones, and glass that were made at about this time. The motifs used to decorate them were both figural and floral. One chalice of gold, ivory, and enamel had sculptured figures at the base of the stem and an enamel frieze of prophets around the cup. Other chalices had nude figures of ivory or *pâte-de-verre* and enameled wheat or grape motifs. A cup of clear crystal with an openwork pattern of silver pine-needles—one of a set of six or more—is in the collection of Maurice Rheims in Paris. Rheims also owns a pectoral cross of silver-gilt, enamel, and mother-of-pearl anemones set within a framework of thorns. These pieces have more decorative than religious significance but as works of art the chalices rank with antique chalices.

During this period, 1890–1893, Lalique executed several curious pieces including a small head of John the Baptist, a *cire perdue* panel representing a centaur and a centauress, and several vases of glass of various colors. Before Lalique moved to the rue Thérèse atelier he had been busy to a great extent with the execution of diamond-set pieces for the better known jewelry firms of Paris. Now with enlarged quarters and the assistance of several workmen he could develop his passion for enameling and his ability as a sculptor and a glassmaker.

Lalique's first glass objects were exhibited in the Salon of 1895. Among these pieces was an oval cameo of a nude woman combing her tresses. In 1896 Lalique executed a large brooch with colored crystallizations of landscape and snow-capped trees called "L'Hiver" for the Russian nobility. The theme of this piece was repeated at least once in a pendant in blue and white enamel on gold which is now in the Museum für Kunst und Gewerbe, Hamburg, Germany.

Lalique's imaginative novel color combinations and shapes and new techniques brought about a revolution in the design of jewelry, which together with the excellence of his design and workmanship made Lalique one of the leading figures in the field of Art Nouveau. Lalique remained faithful to tradition in his designs. Although the subject matter was drawn from nature, he drew upon strange or eerie aspects—the coils of writhing snakes, insects with the torso of a woman, a green lizard with gaping mouth twisted around a flacon, a beetle clutching a fly, or a huge bizarre cock's head with its beak grasping a large diamond. The materials too were dramatic and revolutionary. Lalique often rejected the traditional diamond, emerald, or ruby in favor of semi-precious stones—the opal, jade, coral, amethyst, crystal and chrysolite, combined with colorful enamel and *pâte-de-verre* in various colors. Color, design, and workmanship were always more important to Lalique than precious materials. In addition to gold and silver Lalique used iron, copper, aluminum, brass, ivory, enamel, and mother-of-pearl. His models inspired by nature—the animal and vegetable world including flowers, trees, peacocks, serpents, and insects—were used again and again in his original fantastic designs.

Early brooches and pendants included swans, peacocks, serpents, fish, dragonflies, butterflies, bees, birds, rooster heads, and lizards. The motifs from the botanical world included iris, pond lilies, poppies, orchids, roses, violets, fuchsias, thistles, cow parsley, grapes and grape vines, and pine cones and branches. The pine seemed to be a special favorite with Lalique. There are several pendants with women's heads of ivory or chrysolite surrounded by frames of green enamel pine cones. Pine cones also formed the motif for rings; a watch was ornamented with enamel pine cones, and when Lalique built his own house and atelier the doorway was ornamented with a sculptured pine tree and a wrought iron balcony of pine branches. Grapes, berries, and various fruits were also favorite motifs. However, the most characteristics motif of Lalique jewelry was the nude. Full length nude figures centered pendants and brooches and several nude figures were often entwined with gold, enamel, and semi-precious stones such as opals. There were strange figures of Salomés and Salammbôs of Flaubert and Gustave Moreau, nymphs and other figures from mythology and legend, as well as the modern nudes of Art Nouveau with their flowing tresses. Sculptured heads of ivory or semi-precious stones, such as agate, set in Art Nouveau swirled line designs were exhibited by Lalique in 1898. One corsage ornament has a sculptured agate head with flowing tresses of gold ornamented with flowers centered with small diamonds and a comb of ivory has a draped figure of ivory set among garlands of gold flowers accented with enamel and diamonds.

Although nature and Art Nouveau seem to dominate the designs of Lalique jewelry there were other important influences. Lalique had studied the history of ornament and knew the decorative arts of ancient as well as modern art. The Renaissance influence was important in some of the brooches made in the 1890s and this influence is illustrated in a brooch and pendant exhibited at the Paris Salon of 1895. These pieces had outlines of Renaissance bandwork and the brooch with gold, opals, and amethysts has a figure of a classic nude.

The Egyptian influence on Lalique was especially important and many of the pieces of early jewelry were of Egyptian inspiration. A page of original sketches in *Art et Décoration,* (1897), includes a *flacon* of lotus design and a diadem with borders of Egyptian winged figures and geometric motifs. Enamel borders of Egyptian motifs are also seen on pendants, combs, bracelets, and diadems. A corsage exhibited at the Exhibition of 1900 in Paris was ornamented with a band of scarabs.

Lalique was also fascinated by the groups of veiled and nude figures in Roman and Pompeiian frescoes and he used these figures in plaques of ivory and *pâte-de-verre* in his pendants and brooches. These groups of classic figures were later used on Lalique's glass pendants and on the covers of small glass boxes. Lalique's jewelry also shows the influence of Arabian, Assyrian, and Oriental art; from Merovingian sources came the use of cabochon stones.

Much of Lalique's early jewelry was concentrated on articles for the adornment of women. In addition to brooches, rings, bracelets, pendants, necklaces, belts, corsages, and collars there were diadems and even hat pins and hair pins. One of the articles that Lalique made in his early period was the comb. There are numerous examples of ivory and horn combs with top ornaments of gold, enamel, and precious and semi-precious stones. Motifs on combs included butterflies, bats, nude figures, angels, and a forest scene in enamel. One comb of horn with a large enamel pansy is called "Pensée Fanée," but the most elaborate comb designs were the figures of the Three Graces, bees and a honeycomb, and a peacock.

Between 1891 and 1894 Lalique made an important group of jewels for Sarah Bernhardt which were worn in her roles of "Iseyl," "Gismonda," and "Théodora." These included diadems, collars, and belts of large size and ornate decoration since they were to be seen at a distance. They were made of silver, semi-precious stones, brass, and even aluminum. Lalique also designed stage jewels for Mme Bartet in her role of Bérénice. One large diadem of aluminum had a border of the winged figure of Isis, lotus flowers, and five medallions with scenes of the life of courtesans sculptured in ivory bas-reliefs. These theatrical jewels were greatly admired and created good publicity for

Lalique. He also made many jewels such as collars, necklaces, and diadems for important titled women of France, Russia, Italy, Spain, and England.

In 1894 Lalique exhibited an ivory bas-relief in the Salon de la Societé des Artistes Français. He also engraved several metals at this time. In the Salon of 1896 Lalique exhibited a group of jewelry, several vases, and an important coffre, "Le Triomphe de la Richesse," which had figures of men and women in bronze relief as handles. The most unique exhibit was a bracelet of horn, since it was the first time this material had been used in any except barbarian jewelry.

However, the most important exhibition of Lalique jewelry was at the Exposition Universelle of 1900 in Paris. The articles were displayed in a vitrine constructed with a grille of iron accented with female bronze figures. This grille served as a background screen in front of which the jewels were displayed on a ground of white moiré silk. Lambrequins of gray were appliqued with velour bats. The rug and the draperies were of gray and on the wall at the back was a large painting by Georges Picard which represented small sylphs frolicking by moonlight among the trees at the border of a lake. A mirror reflected two huge bronze serpents. In this spectacular setting Lalique exhibited twenty horn combs ornamented with enamel, opals, amethysts, and chrysoprase; and a variety of collars and diadems. A dramatic corsage ornament with enamel serpents out of whose mouths cascaded ropes of baroque pearls was an important piece. There was also a brooch with nudes of ivory surrounded by enamel snakes. An ornament in the shape of a cock's head held an immense yellow diamond in its beak and a large dragonfly, with wings of translucent enamel scintillating with rose diamonds, had a bust and head of a woman. This group of oversized fantastic objects was the crowning point of Lalique's career as a goldsmith.

Looking at the jewels shown in this exhibit leaves no doubt that Lalique represented a unique and important position in the history of jewelry. His dramatic conception of subject matter that could transform a sketch from nature into a surrealistic fantasy, his breath-taking color schemes executed in transparent *plique à jour*, and his ability as a sculptor in miniature entitle Lalique to the rank of genius. This exhibition was such a sensation and the demand for Lalique jewelry became so great that Lalique was obliged to take on several collaborators. The two names that merit mention at this time according to Henri Vever were a young sculptor named Hoffmann and Chardon, a talented designer. It is also known that both Alphonse Mucha and Eugène Feuillâtre at one time worked with Lalique. Lalique himself worked in many techniques including ceramics, enamel, glass painting, *pâte-de-verre* and engraving. At one time he registered a *poinçon* and a stamp which he used in addition to the "R.LALIQUE" stamp in block letters with which he marked the majority of the pieces of his jewelry, although early pieces are often engraved "Lalique" or "R.Lalique" in script.

In Lalique's transition from jewelry to glass he included glass in many pieces of jewelry with elaborate and expensive settings. Glass plaquettes similar to those of ivory which Lalique made early in his career were at first carved by hand but later the designs were molded and mass-produced. These molded versions of various shapes with designs of nude and draped figures and garlands were so successful that they were continued long after Lalique had shifted the emphasis of his business to mass-produced glassware. In the earlier pieces the glass was often frosted or opaline and bracelets and necklaces continued to be made in both colored and colorless crystal; later glass pendants were only made in colorless glass.

There were oval, round, and heart-shaped pendants. From 150 to 200 of each oval design were made in colorless crystal. The designs included sirens, a figurine with wings, a figurine swinging on a floral rope, a figurine with a scarf over her face and a figurine with a scarf *de dos*. There was also an oval pendant with a design of molded fuchsias, lily of the valley, and mistletoe and one with clover leaves. Round pendants were made in the following designs: "2 Figurines et Fleurs," "3 Papillons" (butterflies), and "2 Perruches" (parakeets). There were also attractive heart-shaped pendants with beaded edges and molded cupid figurines with wings, figurines with flowers, and a heart-shaped pendant with molded swans. The figures on these pendants are molded into the underside of the glass, the transparent surfaces of blank purity being hollowed out by light modeling. This type of work is representative of much of Lalique's early work as a glassmaker. "R.Lalique" in block letters is engraved on the edge of these pieces. Although in the 1890s Lalique used glass for cups, vases, and bowls with mountings of metal and enamel, it was not until after 1900 that glass was increasingly used in his jewelry. Some pieces were frosted and ivory-toned in simulation of ivory.

Glass beads in the shape of leaves and flowers were attached to gold chains. These necklaces were made in both colored and colorless glass and judging from the numbers which were recorded in the 1932 Lalique catalogue they must have been very popular. Necklaces with twelve round and oval beads were made in colored glass. A necklace with beads in the form of ivy leaves was made in both colored and colorless glass. Necklaces with lily of the valley motifs were made in various lengths in colored glass. There were also short necklaces with larger glass motifs. A necklace with sixty beads of dahlia motif was manufactured in vast quantity in colored and colorless glass. The zig-zag Art Deco motif was also popular. As listed in the 1932 catalogue 900 of these necklaces were available in colorless glass and 1,000 in colored glass. A necklace composed of dahlias and roundels was also popular. Necklaces with *décors divers* were also available and there were necklaces of molded ferns and lotus flowers.

Extendable bracelets were made to match many of the necklaces. Bracelets were also made in many other designs of molded beads including cherries, palmettes, ferns, fish, cocks, tomtits, sparrows, griffons, castles, and suns. All of these bracelets were made in both colored and colorless glass and in quantities of hundreds of each design. A bracelet of roundels with enameling was available in large quantity in both colored and colorless glass.

For those collectors who cannot afford the one of a kind pieces of Lalique's early enamel and gem jewelry these later mass-produced glass necklaces, pendants, and bracelets are available and are also again in fashion.

Pendant of Renaissance design. Lalique, 1895. (Henri Vever, *La Bijouterie Française au XIXe Siècle*, III.)

Comb with bat motif and moonstones.
Lalique, 1900. (Art et Décoration, 1900.)

Corsage ornament. Head of
sculptured agate, flowing hair of
gold ornamented with flowers of
diamonds. Lalique. Salon 1898.
(Henri Vever, *La Bijouterie
Française au XIXe Siècle*, III.)

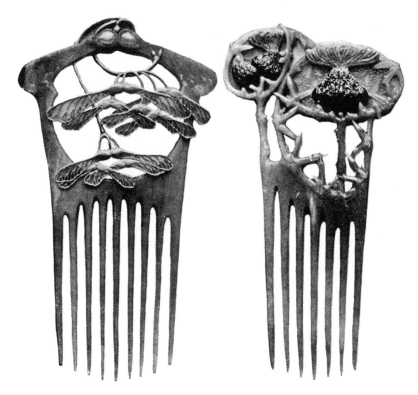

Two combs with plant and insect motifs
enriched with enamel. Lalique c.1900.
(Art et Décoration, 1900.)

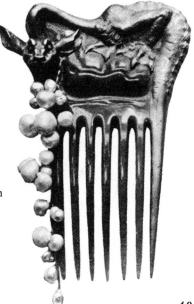

Comb, bee design ornamented with
enamel. Lalique, 1900. (Art et
Décoration, 1902.)

Pendant, grey, black and orange enamel
and gold leaves and woman's head.
Stamped "Lalique" c.1900 (The
Metropolitan Museum of Art, Gift of
Albert M. Kohn, 1910.)

Left, Sculptured peacock, metalwork
and enamel. Lalique c.1895-1900.
(Art et Décoration, 1900.)

Opposite, Gold chain with
conventionalized daisy motifs decorated
with colored enamel and brilliants.
Engraved "R. Lalique." c.1900. (The
Metropolitan Museum of Art, Edward
C. Moore, Jr. Gift, 1924.)

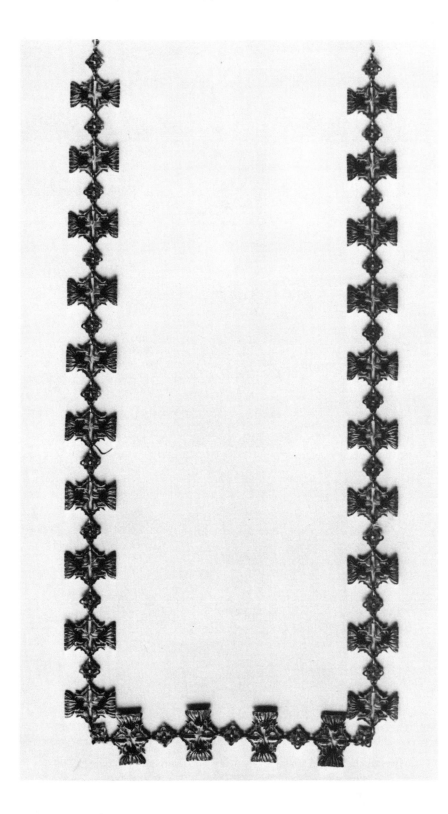

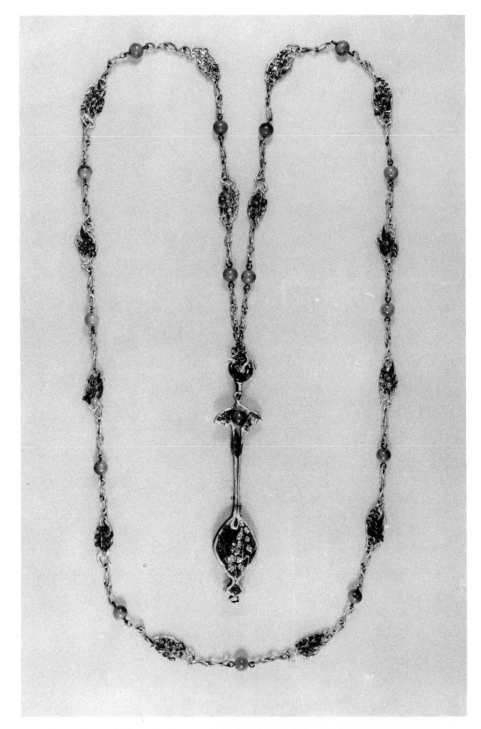

Lorgnette and chain, gold, enamel, jade, glass and diamonds. Lalique, c.1900.
(The Metropolitan Museum of Art, Gift of Mrs. J. G. Phelps Stokes, 1965.)

22

Pendant and chain, lilac motif. Gold, diamonds, enamel and intaglio on glass. Stamped "Lalique." 1905-1910. (The Metropolitan Museum of Art, Gift of Miss Mary F. Failing, 1944, offered in memory of Henrietta Ellison Failing.)

Serpent corsage ornament, blue and green enamel. Lalique, Paris Exposition, 1900. (Henri Vever, *La Bijouterie Française au XIXe Siècle*, III.)

Cock's head comb, enamel, gold and stones. Lalique, Paris Exposition, 1900. (Art et Décoration, 1900.)

Pendant. Female head in crystal, with silver hair, poppies and suspended baroque pearl. Signed "Lalique" in block letters. Gulbenkian Collection. (*Connoisseur*, August, 1971.)

Insect-shaped pendant of crystal, sapphires, diamonds and moonstone. Signed "Lalique." Gulbenkian Collection. (*Connoisseur*, August, 1971.)

Pendant brooch modelled with a
woman's head enclosed in helmet of
gold leaves enamelled in pale and
dark green, hung with a baroque
pearl. Stamped "Lalique." c.1900.
(Sotheby & Co. Sale, March 9,
1970.)

Gold brooch with blue and white
glass poppies. Stems with diamonds
and buds and leaves in opaque
turquoise blue enamel. Hung with
aquamarine. Stamped "Lalique."
c.1895. (Sotheby & Co. Sale,
March 9, 1970.)

Bracelet of oriental design. Silver
chased with dragons enamelled in
pale blue and gilt. Stamped
"Lalique." c.1900. (Sotheby & Co.
Sale, March 9, 1970.)

Tortoise shell comb with orchid in ivory, gilt metal, enamel and brilliants. Lalique. c.1900. (The Walters Art Gallery.)

Necklace with lion and tooth motifs in gilt metal and tortoise shell.
Lalique, 1895-1898. (The Walters Art Gallery.)

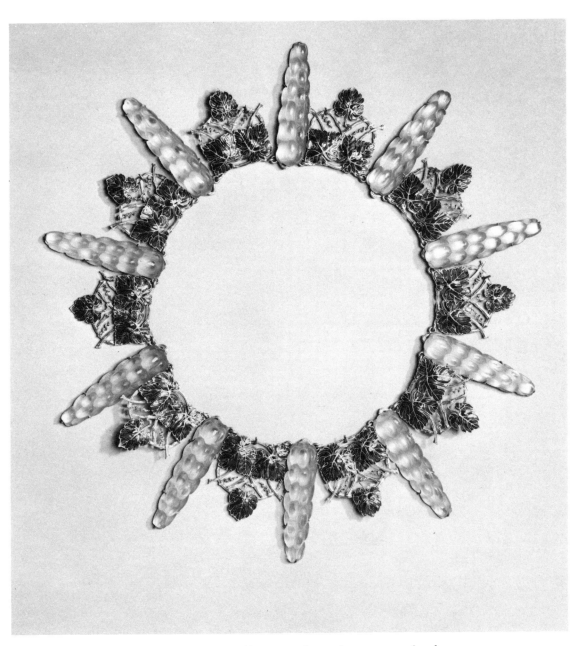

Necklace of grapes and leaves in gilt metal, green enamel and green glass. Lalique. c.1900. (The Walters Art Gallery.)

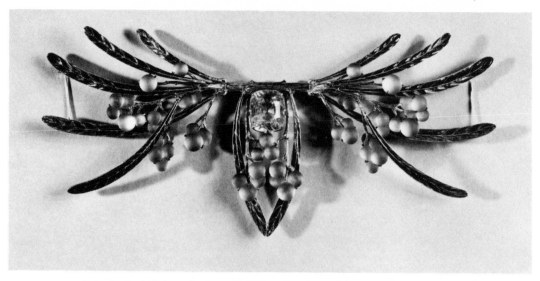

Ornament of gilt metal, glass, enamel and topaz. Lalique. c.1900.
(The Walters Art Gallery.)

Pansy brooch in gilt metal, glass and enamel with sapphire in center.
Lalique. c.1900. (The Walters Art Gallery.)

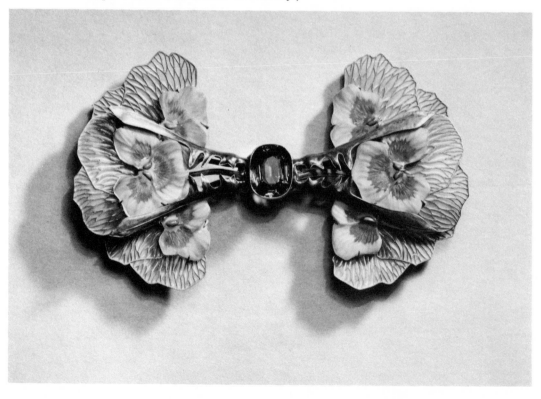

Pendant medallion on black silk cord with seed pearls. Figures of two nudes and blossoms molded on under side of glass. Mark "R. Lalique." c.1930-1935. (The Minneapolis Institute of Arts.)

Necklace with pendant in form of ivory nude standing among wisteria blossoms, of gold, enamel and topaz. Lalique. c.1902. (The Walters Art Gallery.)

Cup of alabaster, with figures of glass and bronze ornamented with grape and vine motif. (International Studio, 1905.)

Cup in ivory, enamels and gold with sculptured figures at base. Lalique. c.1900-1905. (International Studio, 1905.)

Decorative Glass Work

T HE MOST IMPORTANT PIECES OF LALIQUE GLASS FOR THE collector are the vases. Between 150 and 200 different vase designs were made. The majority of the ornate large

GLASS VASES vases are no longer manufactured. For this reason and for artistic value and beauty of their designs these are the most sought after by collectors. Many of the vases are in the decorative Art Deco style, some in the later geometric patterns, but Lalique being of the older generation of designers was too established to completely change his taste and conception of design and thus he continued to favor many of the motifs of Art Nouveau. However as time went on the linear languid flowers of Art Nouveau such as the water lily, iris, and convolvulus were seen to change to formalized roses, dahlias, and sunflowers; the sinuous curves were banished in favor of stylized conventional designs. Gazelles, antelopes, birds, and sirens with flowing hair were popular motifs, and leaves, shells, fish, birds, and insects were arranged in Art Deco spirals. Vibrant colors later replaced the earlier smoky blues, ambers, and opalines and finally the designs were influenced by cubistic Art Deco designs of abstract ovals, squares, and zig-zags.

Some of the earliest Lalique vases were made by the *cire perdue* or lost wax casting process. This allowed for the reproduction of delicate and intricate detail and the results depended upon the skill of the craftsman. Such vases which are unique and few in number may have been executed by Lalique himself. They are accordingly the most valuable Lalique pieces.

Lalique *cire perdue* vases were in clear unpolished glass with tints of green, brown or other light tones. These vases were of leaf designs, nude figures with foliage, and with dragonfly and fish motifs. There is also an early unpolished Lalique vase with a band of dancing cherubs. They are marked with the engraved signature "R.Lalique," "R.Lalique France," and also with the engraved block letter signature "R.Lalique." The majority of the *cire perdue* pieces were early and were made between 1902 and 1913.

The most popular mass-produced Lalique vases were made in great numbers and should thus be available to the collector today. Here is a list of some of the most desirable vases with information about them taken from the 1932 "Catalogue des Verreries de René Lalique."

No. 875   "Antilopes émailleé" (A round vase with short neck and cabochons of clear glass against a background of engraved and enameled antelopes) c. 1925–1926. In 1932 2,000 were available in *blanc* and 2,200 in *couleur.*

No. 876   "Perruches" (Round vase with groups of paired parakeets in relief in tree branches) In 1932 there were 1,000 *blanc* and 1,200 *couleur* available.

No. 877   "Grande boule, lierre" (Spheroid shaped vase with bold pattern of ivy leaves) 2,000 *blanc* and 2,400 *couleur* listed in 1932 Lalique Catalogue.

No. 961 "Cluny" (Spheroid shaped vase blown in mold with bronze handles of masque design) 2,850 *couleur* listed in 1932 Lalique Catalogue. First made c. 1925.

No. 962 "Senalis" (Spheroid shaped vase blown in mold with bronze handles of Stylized leaves) 2,750 listed in *couleur* in 1932 Lalique Catalogue. *c.* 1925.

No. 1024 "Pétrarque" (Vase with heavy oval handles of molded flowers) 1,200 *blanc* and 1,500 *couleur* listed in 1932 Lalique Catalogue.

No. 1030 "Margaret" (Vase with heavy square handles of molded flowers) 900 *blanc* and 1,000 *couleur* listed in 1932 Lalique Catalogue.

No. 964 "Oranges émaillé" (Spheroid shaped vase with large oranges and enameled leaves) 1,650 *blanc* and 1,850 *couleur* listed in 1932 Lalique Catalogue.

No. 993 "Bellecour" (Vase with four frosted figures of birds at top of neck) 1,200 *blanc* and 1,400 *couleur* listed in 1932 Lalique Catalogue.

No. 997 "Bacchantes" (Straight-sided vase with figures of molded nudes) 1,500 *blanc* and 1,650 *couleur* listed in 1932 Lalique Catalogue. Vase still in production.

No. 883 "Méplat, Sirènes" (Oval vase with panels of nude figures and stopper of nude figurine) 1,250 *blanc* and 1,400 *couleur* listed in 1932 Lalique Catalogue.

No. 878 "4 Masques" (Round vase with short neck and four medallions of masques and foliage in relief) *c.* 1911. 1,300 *blanc* and 1,500 *couleur* listed in 1932 Lalique Catalogue.

No. 880 "Vase 2 Anneux" (A tall urn-shaped vase available with molded handles in choice of figures of scarabs, lizards, or pigeons suspended from glass loops at top of vase shoulder) 1,200 *blanc* and 1,400 *couleur* listed in 1932 Lalique Catalogue.

No. 1048   "Naïades" (Bowl with a base of molded figures of nude water nymphs) 2,000 *blanc* and 2,200 *couleur* listed in 1932 Lalique Catalogue.

No. 1054   "Nadica" (Vase with pair of molded water nymphs whose bodies extend into handles for vase) 2,800 *blanc* and 3,500 *couleur* listed in 1932 Lalique Catalogue.

No. 998   "Alicante" (Round shouldered vase with short neck and design of large parrot heads in relief) 975 *blanc* and 1,150 *couleur* listed in 1932 Lalique Catalogue.

No. 999   "Oran" (Vase with molded design of camellias) 1,000 *blanc* and 1,100 *couleur* listed in 1932 Lalique Catalogue.

No. 1015   "Salmonides" (Round vase with short neck and all-over design of molded fish) 900 *blanc* and 1,000 *couleur* listed in 1932 Lalique Catalogue.

No. 1057   "Chrysanthème" (Covered vase with stopper of wood) 1,500 *blanc* listed in 1932 Lalique Catalogue.

No. 1071   "Merles" (Vase with design of blackbirds in cut glass) 1,300 *blanc* listed in 1932 Lalique Catalogue.

In addition to the above listed vases there are others that are particularly interesting because of their subject or fine design and these are in demand with collectors today. These include the well-known

No. 893   "Archers" (An oval vase with short neck and a design in relief of nude males hunting tropical birds) Height 10 inches. It was first made c. 1923 in *blanc* and smoky colors. 750 *blanc* and 850 *couleur* were listed in the 1932 Lalique Catalogue.

No. 896   "Serpent" (A vase with molded design of a coiled snake) First made c. 1923. 500 *blanc* and 550 *couleur* were listed in the 1932 Lalique Catalogue.

No. 892   "Gros Scarabées" (Spheroid vase with short neck and an allover design of scarabs or beetles in relief) 800 *blanc* and 900
couleur were listed in the 1932 Lalique Catalogue.

No. 919   "Aras" (An oval vase with a molded design of tropical birds
and cherries) 550 *blanc* and 650 *couleur* listed in the 1932
Lalique Catalogue.

No. 925   "Poissons" (A large round vase with an allover design of
goldfish in relief) 525 *blanc* and 625 *couleur* were listed in
the 1932 Lalique Catalogue. A similar design was on a smaller
vase called "Formose" No. 934.

No. 966   "Tortues" (An oval vase with short neck and an allover
design of large molded turtles) First made *c.* 1926. 525 *blanc*
and 625 *couleur* were listed in the 1932 Lalique Catalogue.

No. 977   "Sophora" (A spheroid vase with short neck and a design of
a leafy vine) First made *c.* 1926. 375 *blanc* and 450 *couleur*
were listed in the 1932 Lalique Catalogue.

There were numerous vases with leaf designs including the large spheroid
vase with short neck with molded veined leaves called "Charmille" (No. 978)
and "Languedoc" (No. 1021), a vase with triangular leaves and rimmed lip
which was available in both colorless and colored glass. "Armorique" (No.
1000) was a vase of artichoke shape with molded artichoke leaves. This was
available in both colorless and colored glass. One small vase had an allover
relief pattern of palm leaves, another "Epicea" or spruce, and an important
large vase, "Acanthes" (No. 902), was of oval form with small short neck
and had a design of acanthus leaves in relief. It was available in both colorless and colored glass. There was a panel of molded leaves on each side of
"Honfleur" (No. 994) a vase first made *c.* 1926-1927.

The shell was also a favorite design on Lalique vases. There was a
decanter in the shape of a clam shell and a round vase, "Escargot" (No.
931), was molded in the design of a snail shell. It was made in both colorless

and colored glass. "Coquilles" (No. 932), was a small upright rectangular vase with rounded shoulders and a short neck. It had a relief design of scallop shells. "Dordogne" (No. 1001) was a squat oval vase with borders of protruding molded snail shells. It was available in both colorless and colored glass.

Undoubtedly the most characteristic and most desirable of all Lalique vases are those with nude figures either molded in the design of the vase or applied as handles or stoppers. In addition to the better known vases such as "Sirènes," "Danaïdes," "Nadica," and "Bacchantes" there were vases with panels of figurines such as "6 Figurines et Masques" (No. 886) which has panels of figurines in relief alternating with panels of plain glass. This was a large vase made in both colorless and colored glass. There was also a large goblet with six panels of veiled figurines and a covered vase with panels of caryatides. "12 Figurines avec Bouchon" (No. 914) is ornamented with figures of nude women and has a nude figurine for a stopper; 600 *blanc* and 700 *couleur* were available in the 1932 Catalogue. An early funnel-shaped vase ornamented with oval medallions of nudes in relief was called "Camées"; 900 *blanc* and 1,000 *couleur* were listed in the 1932 Lalique Catalogue.

A delightful round vase with short neck and handle of nudes holding garlands of flowers is called "Ronsard" (No. 982). This vase was first made c. 1926–1927 in both colorless and colored glass. A similar vase "Bouchardon" (No. 981) was made at about the same date and both were illustrated in *Mobilier et Décoration* in 1927.

There are also attractive small vases. A bowl with a base of sculptured nude wrestlers is called "Lutteurs." It was made in both *blanc* and *couleur*. "Courges," a gourd-shaped vase in Art Nouveau style, is slightly reminiscent of the gourd vases of Gallé and Daum. It was an early vase, but 300 *blanc* and 350 *couleur* were listed in the 1932 Lalique Catalogue. "Ceylan" was a jar with pairs of parakeets in relief. It is most often seen in a pale blue opalescent color although it was made in other colors and also in colorless glass. Another small but highly desirable vase was "Lièvres" (No. 942) a round vase with short neck ornamented with leaves and a band of running hares in relief. This was available in both *blanc* and *couleur*.

Many of the designs of Lalique are influenced by Art Nouveau and there are other designs that are definitely Art Deco in style but above all else Lalique glass is unmistakably French. The flowing hair of the nude figurines and sea nymphs, the streams of water flowing from the vases held by the nudes on the vase "Danaïdes" and the stylized roses and antelope motifs are all themes of the more graceful type of Art Deco. However, there are also many designs of zig-zags, stepped shapes and geometric motifs that relate to later Art Deco and the influence of Cubism. The vase "Soleil," a flower with sun-like rays made in clear glass with enamel, and the vase "Picardie," with sunken designs of huge daisies with rayed petals, were both inspired by Art Deco. This latter vase first exhibited in 1927–1928 continued to be available in 1932 in both colorless and colored glass. Engraved spirals decorate the rare small vase "Méduse" and applied spirals of molded design are on the sides of several vases.

The vases most characteristic of Art Deco are those with molded and enameled zig-zag designs relating to Indian art. In 1925 Lalique exhibited the vase "Tourbillons," which had a large scroll design. It was made in clear glass sometimes accented with enamel. A group of small vases with allover Art Deco designs of ducks, cocks, chamois, and stylized leaves were available in colored glass in 1932.

The identification of Lalique glass is not difficult because all pieces are marked. Although glass of similar designs made by Sabino, Genet & Michon, and other glassmakers such as André Hunebelle show the signs of Lalique influence there has been no direct plagiarism of Lalique designs or marks.

Lalique glass was halfway between commercial and studio production and although it was mass-produced the high standard of quality and the distinctive touch and design were maintained for many years. Lalique glass was produced by a number of techniques including the use of fluoridic acids, polishing on the wheel, and considerable handwork.

Lalique glass for collectors dates from 1900 when the first experimental pieces were made until the death of René Lalique in 1945. In February-March, 1933, a retrospective exhibition of Lalique's work was put on at the Pavillon de Marsan of The Musée des Arts Décoratifs and the catalogue of this exhibit records the jewelry, sculpture, and glass from vases to fountains. Included was the early vase with dragonfly handles, the owl vase, and a unique vase with peacock figure stopper called "Verrier de Génie." There were also decorative lighted glass panels with horses and riders and a peacock panel. "Christ on Cross" and a Madonna were representative of Lalique's religious glass. However the catalogue of this exhibit is of little assistance in dating the vases available to the collector today since many of the pieces were one of a kind pieces.

Although there were trade catalogues put out by Lalique the only ones available for study are the lighting catalogues distributed by Breves Galleries, London, in 1928, and the large Lalique Catalogue of 1932. The latter catalogue lists and illustrates the pieces of decorative glass then available, whether the pieces were made in "blanc" or "couleur" glass and how many pieces were then in stock. This information gives little aid in dating a piece of glass for many of the articles in the Catalogue were first made earlier and also continued in production after 1932. The approximate dates of some articles can be traced in periodicals or advertisements. Any piece thus traced must have been made before the date of the publication of the article or illustration. The Lalique signature also does not definitely establish the date of a piece since various signatures were used at the same time. Also similar vases have been seen signed in script or block capitals impressed or engraved.

The signatures were "R.Lalique," engraved in script; "R.Lalique" engraved in block letters, and "R.Lalique" or "R.Lalique France" in molded block letters. A rare signature is "Lalique" in block letters molded with the base of the "L" elongated to form a base for the rest of the letters. Lalique glass is usually marked on the bottom or on the base of a piece near the bottom and it is often marked in both places and in a script as well as a block signature. The signature "Lalique" or "R.Lalique" engraved in round letters is found in the body of a vase, the beetle perfume bottle, on a paperweight, on the statuette "Moyenne Nue" (No. 830), and on a round box with a rooster. A similar rounded signature "R.Lalique" is on many vases. *Cire perdue* pieces are usually signed with engraved block letters or in engraved script which could be Lalique's own signature. When there is a number on a piece it refers to the design as recorded in the Lalique "Catalogue des Verreries de René Lalique" (1932). After 1945, the year of Lalique's death, the mark is "Lalique" without the initial "R." Today Lalique glass is marked "Lalique France" in small pointed script on the bottom or sometimes on the body of the piece. The 1932 Lalique Catalogue uses the words "blanc" and "couleur." "Blanc" however means uncolored not white and "couleur" usually means the whole range of colors from amber to deep reds, blues, and greens.

Early Lalique *cire perdue* experimental pieces are frosty but Lalique also used opalescent glass in his jewelry and there is an opaline bowl of Art Nouveau design dating from 1900. When Lalique started mass production the glass was monotone with smoky opaline tints and with contrasts of clear crystal and soft satin finished glass. The lightly tinted glass was in shades of blue, brown, and peach. The 1932 Catalogue lists the colors as "opale, bleu, vert, brun, etc." Today vases have been found in more than ten different colors including deep dark brown, red, blue, green, turquoise, purple, black, the lighter shades of yellow, amber, gray, and opaline. The darker colors tend toward the opaque. Black is especially popular with present day collectors. Many pieces were available in the whole range of colors and others were only made in clear crystal (blanc). Glass surfaces were clear, translucent, polished and matte or frosted. Enamel and engraved decoration were used in addition to molded patterns. A few pieces were also "taillé" (cut). Present day Lalique glass is generally uncolored crystal and more clinical in appearance.

Collectors are especially interested in pieces of Art Deco design and any unusual pieces. Colored pieces are more in demand than opalescent. Black is most desirable and *cire perdue* pieces in which the wax mold was broken after casting are rare one of a kind pieces. Although still much lower priced than Tiffany and Gallé and his school which preceded it in the Art Nouveau era, Lalique fits in well with the present nostalgia for the 1920's. The opaline pieces with their pale blue opal-like gleam are immediately recognizable and one soon comes to recognize the colors and designs of other pieces. Pieces with a combination of cutting and casting produce a pleasing appearance.

Left, Decanter, clear glass, stained and molded Bacchantian masques. Heart-shaped silver stopper with fruit design. Vase marked with diamond point signature "R. Lalique." Stopper marked "France, Lalique." 1911-1930. (Sotheby's Belgravia Sale, March 8, 1972.)

Below, Water nymph, *cire perdue*. Height, 3 inches. Engraved signature "R. Lalique." c.1910. (John Jesse Gallery.)

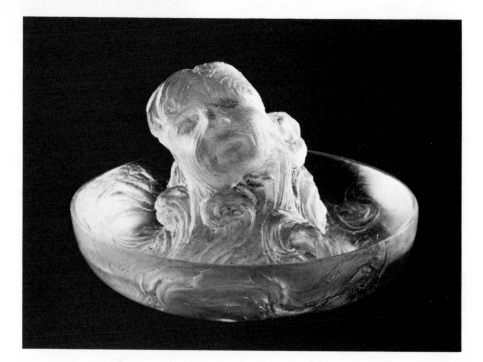

Dragonfly vase with cover, *cire perdue*. c.1910-1913. Signed
"R. Lalique" in block letters engraved on lid. (The Metropolitan
Museum of Art, Edward C. Moore, Jr. Gift, 1924.)

Above, Vase, fish head motif, *cire perdue*. Signed "R. Lalique France F19529." 1902-1912. (Collection Mr. and Mrs. Robert Walker.)

Opposite, Vase, brown color with female figures and foliage. Signed "R. Lalique" in block letters. c.1902-1912. (*Connoisseur*, August, 1971.)

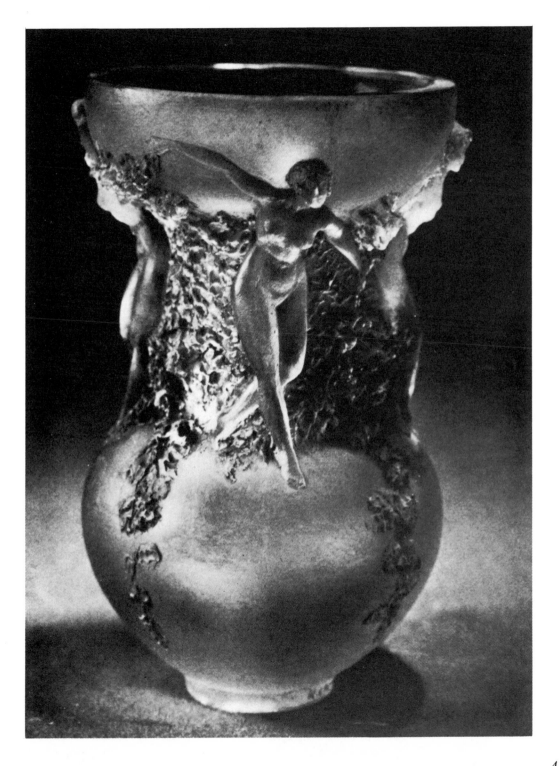

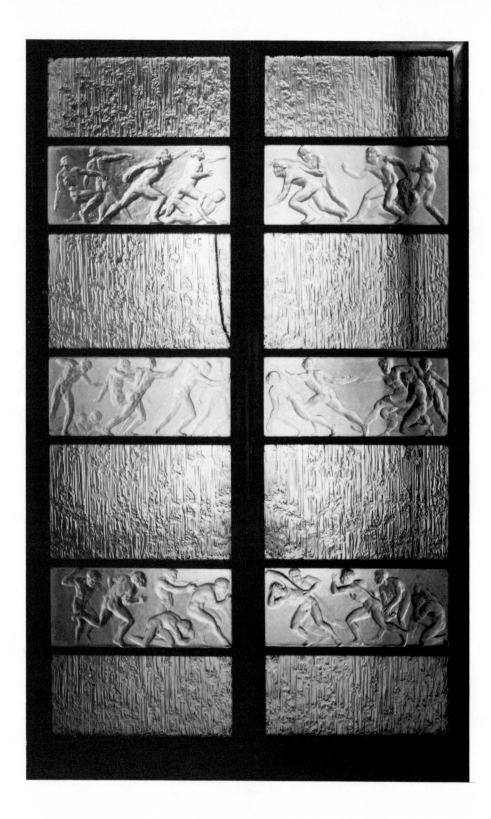

Above, Vase with figures of children and draperies. "R. Lalique." c.1900-1910.
(Musée des Arts Décoratifs.)

Left, Glass door with alternating plaques of nude male figures and greenery.
c.1922. (Gallerie Felix Marcilhac.)

Right, Vase, leaf pattern in greenish-white glass, *cire perdue*. R. Lalique. 1913. (Musée des Arts Décoratifs.)

Below, "Sirens," opalescent glass dish molded with mermaids bathing in spray. Marked "R. Lalique France, No. 3003." Before 1924. (Sotheby's Belgravia Sale, March 28, 1972.)

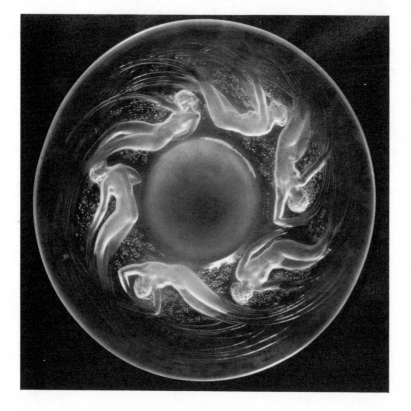

Left, Vase, brownish glass molded and engraved with leaf sprays in relief. Lalique c. 1913-1914. (The Metropolitan Museum of Art, Edward C. Moore, Jr. Gift, 1936.)

Below, Dish "Sirene" with one molded central figure of mermaid. Lalique, c.1925. (The Cooper-Hewitt Museum of Decorative Arts.)

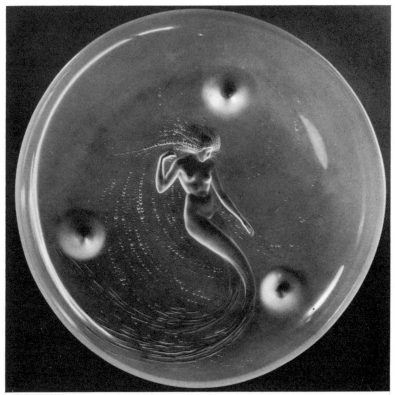

Vase of tear-drop form, trumpet neck,
orange-tinted glass with stylized leaves
part polished in relief against white frosted
ground. Base engraved "R. Lalique France
No. 1014." c.1925. (Sotheby's Belgravia
Sale, June 22, 1973.)

Vase "Tourbillons," amber glass
molded in high relief with motif
of barbed scrolls outlined in black
enamel. Base engraved "R.
Lalique" incised, block letters.
c.1925. (The Cooper-Hewitt
Museum of Decorative Arts.)

Vase "Deux Pigeons," colorless glass with loop handles with figures of pigeons.
(The Metropolitan Museum of Art, Edward C. Moore, Jr., Gift Fund, 1937.)

Vase "Perruches," bluish grey glass pressed in mold. No. 876. Also made in colorless glass. c.1925. (The Metropolitan Museum of Art, Edward C. Moore, Jr. Gift, 1933.)

Vase "Nadica." Clear colorless glass pressed in mold with design of nude sea maidens.
Before 1932. Also made in color. (The Metropolitan Museum of Art, Gift of
Edward C. Moore, Jr. 1936.)

Above left, Vase "Yvelines.".No. 975. Made in both *blanc* and *couleur*. Before 1932. (John Jesse Gallery.)

Above right, Vase "Aigrettes," molded design in dark smoky glass. Height, 10 inches. Also made in clear colorless glass. Before 1932. (The Chrysler Museum at Norfolk.)

Left, Vase, clear colorless glass with decoration of birds in sunk relief. c.1925-1935. (The Metropolitan Museum of Art, Edward C. Moore, Jr. Gift, 1936.)

Vase "Cluny," No. 961. Smoky, transparent glass with
bronze metal masque handles. Height, 10 inches. (The
Chrysler Museum at Norfolk.)

Vase "Marisa." No 1022. All-over design of fish cast in mold and made in both white transparent and colored glass. Height, 9¼ inches. (The Chrysler Museum at Norfolk.)

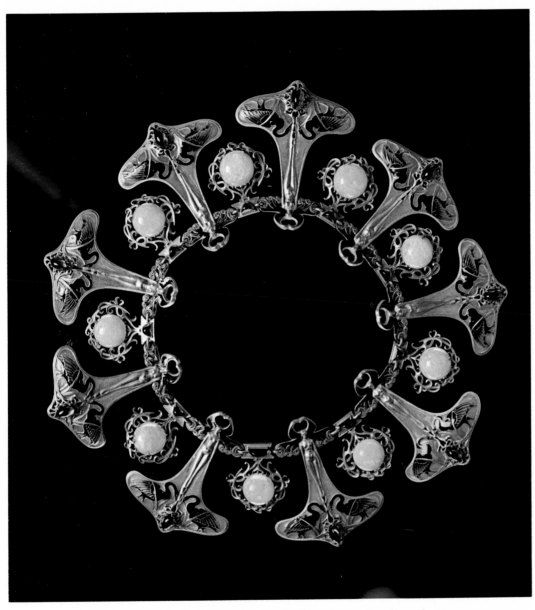

Gold necklace with alternating plaques of gold and enamel nudes and
swans, each with amethyst and opals. Made for Exposition 1900. Stamped
"Lalique." (Collection Lillian Nassau.)

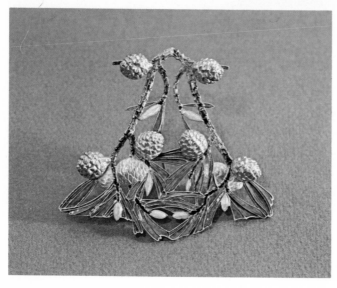

Left, Gold necklace with pendant of blue and white swan. Stamped "Lalique." 1898. (Collection Lillian Nassau.)

Right, Ivory brooch in frame of brown enamel oak twigs and leaves. Stamped "Lalique." c. 1899. (Collection Lillian Nassau.)

Left, Pine cone pendant, gold and enamel. Lalique. c. 1900. (Collection Galerie Felix Marcilhac.)

Left, Necklace of scarabs, gold, enamel, and cabochon stones. (Anonymous Collection.)

Below, Group of Lalique perfume flagons. Left to right: "Amphytrite," shell design, green; "Amphytrite," shell design, blanc; "Serpent," crystal with etched design of serpent and serpent stopper; "Cigales," tall crystal flagon with enamel accents; turquoise bottle with design of tropical birds in relief. Roger et Gallet "Le Jade." Marked "R. L." in moulded letters. (Collection Robert Sistrunk.)

Left, Vase "Serpent," brown-amber. Mark, "R Lalique" in block letters impressed in mould. (Antaeus Gallery Inc.)

Below left, Vase "Druids." Cased emerald green. Mark, rounded script "R Lalique France #937." (Antaeus Gallery Inc.)

Below, Vase "Poissons." Clear orange. Mark, script signature "R Lalique #925." (Antaeus Gallery Inc.)

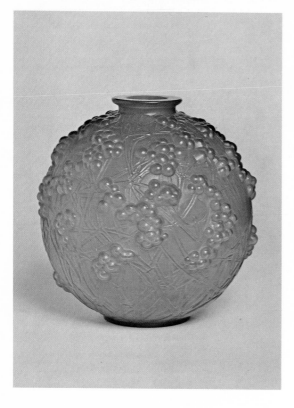

Above, "Penthièvre." #1011. Art Deco design of fish. Mark, "R Lalique France" in script. (Antaeus Gallery Inc.)

Above right, Vase "Monnaie du Pape." Colorless glass with surface patination. Stamped "R Lalique" in block letters. (Antaeus Gallery Inc.)

Right, Vase "Courges." Rare design of pumpkins, pale amethyst glass. Mark, stamped "Lalique" with elongated "L," also engraved "Lalique" in small pointed script. (Antaeus Gallery Inc.)

Vase "Formosa." Design of gold fish in cased yellow glass. Mark, "R Lalique" in block letters. Same vase in red marked "R Lalique France" in script. (Antaeus Gallery Inc.)

Vase "Bacchantes." Opalescent design of nudes cast in mould. Mark, engraved signature "R Lalique" in script. (Antaeus Gallery Inc.)

Vase "Pigeons." Pale sapphire blue with white enamel. Mark, engraved signature "R Lalique" in script. (Antaeus Gallery Inc.)

Two vases. *Left*, "Méduse." Green. Design of spirals. Mark, "R Lalique France" in script. *Right*, red vase with small neck, design of brambles. Mark, "R Lalique" in block letters impressed in mould. (Antaeus Gallery Inc.)

Vase "Lagamar." Art Deco design in black enamel and white frosting. Mark, "R Lalique" engraved in block letters. (Antaeus Gallery Inc.)

Vase "Bouchardon." Frosted platinum grey blown in mould. Mark, "R Lalique" pressed in mould and "R Lalique France" in script. (Antaeus Gallery Inc.)

Vase "Pierrefonds" with open scroll design in handles. No. 990. Made in both colorless and color. Lalique. c.1927-8. (The Corning Museum of Glass.)

Jardinière "Saint Hubert." Handles with antelopes. Height 5¼ inches. Made in white clear glass before 1927. (The Chrysler Museum at Norfolk.)

Vase "Bacchantes." Design of nude figures made in mold. Before 1932. Still being made. (John Jesse Gallery.)

Vase "Poivre" (pepper berries), dark grey transparent glass. Mark, "R. Lalique" in block letters. (Sybarites Gallery Inc.)

Vase "Gros Scarabées." No. 892. Deep red-orange. Before 1932. Mark "R. Lalique France" in rounded script. (The Columbus Gallery of Fine Arts.)

LALIQUE

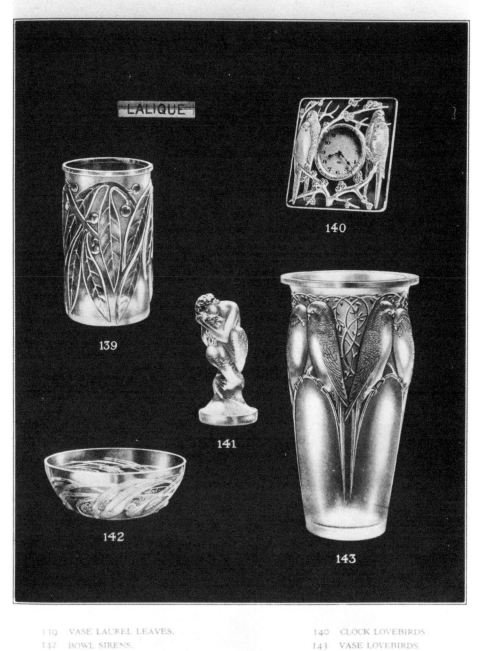

139   VASE LAUREL LEAVES.   140   CLOCK LOVEBIRDS.
142   BOWL SIRENS.   143   VASE LOVEBIRDS.
              141   PAPER WEIGHT SIREN.

Page from Lalique catalogue printed in England before 1932. (John Jesse Gallery.)

62

Vase, grasshopper and grass design. Pressed acid finish and polish glass. Height, 11 inches. Mark, "R. Lalique" in block letters. 1920-1925. (The Toledo Museum of Art.)

Opposite, above: Vase "Dordogne" molded design of shells. Opaque white glass stamped "R. Lalique" in block letters and "R. Lalique" in rounded script. (Sybarites Gallery Inc.)

Opposite, below: Vase with base of two molded cupids. Height 10¾ inches. Mark, etched on bottom, "R. Lalique France." Before 1932. (The Toledo Museum of Art.)

Left, Vase of opalescent glass with decorative border in satin finish relief pattern of flowers. Height, 5⅝ inches. (The Toledo Museum of Art.)

Right, Vase "Camargue." Frosted and clear glass with four carved plaques with figures of horses. Height, 11⅜ inches. R. Lalique, 1940-1945. (The Toledo Museum of Art.)

Handleless amphora-shaped vase with
molded design of alligators against
background of pineapple branches. Black
glass. Height, 13¼ inches. Signed "R.
Lalique" on bottom edge. c.1920. (William
Rockhill Nelson Gallery of Art.)

Vase, blue glass blown in
mold; fern leaf pattern.
Height, 7 inches. Mark,
"R. Lalique." c.1930. (The
Toledo Museum of Art.)

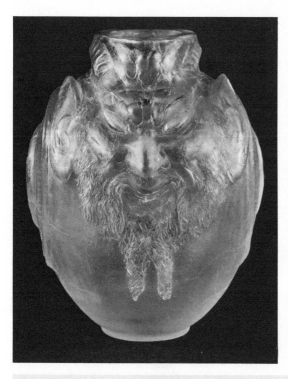

Above, left, Vase in *cire perdue* with molded face of satyr. R. Lalique, c.1922. (Sybarites.)

Above right, Vase in *cire perdue* with molded design of grapes and leaves and head of Bacchus. R. Lalique, c.1922. (Sybarites.)

Left, Vase "Escargot." No. 931. Blue-green glass. Mark, "Lalique," in rounded script. "R. Lalique," in block letters. Before 1932. (Martin Cohen.)

Vase, *cire perdue*. Colorless, pitted unpolished glass. Lalique, 1900-1910.
Mark "R. Lalique" carved in block letters. (Martin Cohen.)

"The Archers" vase. Relief design of men with bows and arrows hunting birds. Colored glass. R. Lalique, c.1925. (Editions Graphiques Ltd.)

Vase "Danaïdes." Relief of nudes with water jars. R. Lalique,
c.1927. No. 972 in 1932 Catalogue. (Editions Graphiques Ltd.)

❧❧ STATUETTES AND DECORATIVE MOTIFS

Lalique had studied sculpture early in his career and became an accomplished sculptor. Throughout the years he continued his interest in the plastic arts. Small ivory and *pâte-de-verre* glass nude figures were often used in his jewelry designs and he continued to use sculpture on his glass vases and other articles. From time to time Lalique was associated with several well-known French sculptors. For a short while he worked in collaboration with the sculptor Gaston Lachaise and created a number of designs incorporating the human figure in molded lightly tinted glass. There were many statuettes of nudes and veiled figures. These figures were very popular and twenty-nine different figures of veiled or nude subjcts were listed in the 1932 Catalogue. The figures were made in several sizes and in different poses. Some were on metal or wooden bases with concealed lighting. The figures included such titles as "Sirènes," Naïade," and a straining figure called "Vitesse" or speed, which was also available as a radiator cap. One of the favorite figures was "Suzanne," a nude holding drapery over her outstretched arms. This figure is now known as "Suzanne au Bain." It is 8¾ inches in height and was made in both colorless and opalescent glass. It has a molded signature "R.Lalique" and the base is engraved "R.Lalique France No. 833." The figure was mounted for electricity. A figure (No. 834) in similar posture but clothed in a sheath was called "Thaïs." It represents a girl in the Art Deco style of the 1920's.

The following statuettes were listed in the 1932 Lalique Catalogue together with the number available in both *blanc* and *couleur* (colorless and colored) :

No. 826   "Statuette joueuse de flûte" (flute player) 1,250 *blanc*: "Statuettes of Four Seasons" Figures of women with appropriate symbols. Motif figures of two birds on a molded arch.

No. 827 "Statuette tête penchée" (inclined head) 1,250 *blanc*, 1,500 *couleur*: Figure enclosed in oval of glass with floral decoration in relief.

No. 828 "Statuette voilée, mains jointes" (veiled nude with hands clasped at neck) *blanc* 750, *couleur* 850.

No. 829 "Statuette moyenne, voilée" (medium sized statuette 350 *blanc*, 400 *couleur*.

No. 830 "Statuette moyenne, nue" (statuette, medium sized, nude) *Blanc* 350, *couleur* 400.

No. 831 "Statuette Sirène (small nude on circular base) *Blanc* 250, *couleur* 275.

No. 832 "Statuette Naïade" (small nude on circular base) *Blanc* 300, *couleur* 350.

No. 833 "Statuette Suzanne" (nude with drapery hanging from outstretched arms) *Blanc* 550, *couleur* 625.

No. 833 "Statuette Suzanne" (on bronze base mounted for electricity) *Blanc* 1,100, *couleur* 1,175.

No. 834 "Statuette Thaïs" *Blanc* 550, *couleur* 625.

No. 834 "Statuette Thaïs" (on bronze base mounted for electricity) *Blanc* 1,100, *couleur* 1,175.

No. 835 "Statuette, grande nue, bras levés" (large standing nude with arms raised over head) *Blanc* 1,350.

No. 835 "Statuette, grande nue" (on base of wood mounted for electricity) *Blanc* 1,750.
"Statuette grande nue, longs cheveux" (large standing nude with flowing hair) On base with molded ivy and wooden stand. *Blanc* 1,900, *couleur* 2,350.

No. 837 "Statuette, Source de la Fontaine" (three different oriental figurines) made in 13 different sizes on wooden base *Blanc* 1,350–1,900.

No. 1160   "Statuette Vitesse" (nude in straining position with hands clasped back of head) *Blanc* 285, *couleur* 325.

No. 1183   "Statuette Chrysis" (nude) *Blanc* 325, *couleur* 350.

Lalique also invented decorative motifs composed of circular or semi-circular pieces of glass about an inch in thickness. These had a design on their back deeply etched in acid. They were mounted on a bronze or wooden base with a concealed electric bulb and the light shone through the glass illuminating the incised design. These decorative pieces are some of the most dramatic and striking pieces made by Lalique. One of the most interesting and characteristic pieces was "Surtout 2 Cavaliers." This etched and frosted intaglio design of two plumed knights on web-footed horses tilting at each other was on an arched form panel of crystal. It was set on a bronze base with a pattern of cobwebs and stems which concealed the light fittings. The piece is 36 inches in length and the glass is engraved "R. Lalique." A piece of similar size was etched with a design of three peacocks. "Oiseau de Feu" (firebird) was another dramatic design. Inspired by the ballet of that name, first performed in Paris in 1917 and repeated through 1917, the plaque was probably designed and first produced during those years. The design is of an exotic feathered bird with the nude torso of a woman. It is set on a bronze base which conceals an electric globe. The glass is engraved "R.Lalique" in block letters.

There were more than thirty different designs of decorative motifs listed in the 1932 Lalique Catalogue. They are as follows:

No. 1100   "Gros Poisson Vagues" (large fish with mouth closed) *Blanc* 2,200, *couleur* 2,450. This was also available mounted on a bronze stand wired for electricity. *Blanc* 2,750, *couleur* 3,000.

No. 1101   "Gros Poisson Algues" (large fish with mouth closed, seaweed decoration) *Blanc* 2,000, *couleur* 2,250. Mounted on bronze base decorated with seaweed and wired for electricity. *Blanc* 2,725, *couleur* 2,975.

No. 1106   "Motif Hirondelles" (Group of three swallows mounted on glass base) *Blanc* 900. Also on bronze base. No. 1,107. *Blanc* 350.

No. 1108   "4 Danseuses" (group of nude dancers mounted on bronze base) *Blanc* 1,200. Also on bronze base mounted for electricity. *Blanc* 1,300.

No. 1109   "Surtout 2 Cavaliers" (centerpiece).Two cavaliers joisting on web-footed horses mounted on bronze base wired for electricity. *Blanc* 8,000.

No. 1110   "3 Paons (three peacocks) Mounted on bronze base wired for electricity. *Blanc* 8,000.

No. 1111   "Oiseau de Feu" (Firebird with exotic feathers and torso of woman) *Blanc* 1,900. Also wired for electricity. *Blanc* 2,450.

Nos. 1149 –1151   "Moineau Fier" Moineau Hardi" "Moineau Timide" (three figures of sparrows in different moods, proud, bold, and timid) *Blanc* 125 each. Satin finished.

Nos. 1154 –1156   "Moineau sur socle ailes croisées, ailes ouvertes, ailes fermées" (sparrow on base with wings crossed, with wings open, with wings closed) On square glass bases. *Blanc* 250 each. Satin finished.

Nos. 1165 –1167   "Moineau coquet" "Moineau sournois" "Moineau moqueur" (three figures of sparrows, coquette, cunning, and jeering) *Blanc* 125 each.

No. 1169   "Surtout Caravelle" (large half circle of glass engraved with galleon with sails unfurled) *Blanc* 10,000. Satin finished.

No. 1175   "Surtout Amours" (centerpiece with figures of lovers) *Blanc* 15,000.

No. 1170   "Surtout Yéso" (large centerpiece with tropical fish swimming among bubbles) *Blanc* 3,000.

No. 1171 –1173   "Surtout Fauvettes, A, B, C" (eight warblers sitting on tree branches. Three different arrangements of birds) On rectangular glass panels. *Blanc* 2,800 each.

No. 1174	"Surtout Nid d'Oiseaux" (small circular panel engraved with scene of two birds feeding small birds in nest) *Blanc* 15,000.
No. 1177	"Surtout Tulipes" (large circular centerpiece engraved with bouquet of tulips) *Blanc* 12,000.
No. 1178	"Vase 2 Anémones" (small round vase with stopper of two anemones) *Blanc* frosted 200. Still being made.
Nos. 1179 –1180	"Anémone ouverte" "Anémone fermée" (single blossoms of flowers in satin finish) *Blanc* 60 each. Still being made.
Nos. 1199 –1200	"Pigeon Liège" "Pigeon Namur" (Figures of pigeons) *Blanc* 450 each.

There were also large frosted figures of quail and after 1932 numerous figures of other birds including owls and animals such as elephants, bison, fox, dogs, and a sitting and crouching cat. The early figures were sculptured in stylized planes. Some figures were engraved showing the animals' fur but later figures show only the form of the animal in frosted glass. Animal figures were made in several sizes in both clear and satin finish glass. They do not seem to have been made in colored glass. Animal figures proved so successful that they were continued for many years and some of the original figures are still being produced while new figures are also being introduced.

Lalique designed a number of religious plaques including several different interpretations of Christ on the Cross, the Virgin and Child, and one of St. Thérèse. There was also a "Medaille Jeanne d'Arc." Religious subjects also included a scene of The Last Supper which was enclosed in a border of symbolic wheat and grapes and a Madonna and Child with a frame of satin finish angels in relief. Lalique exhibited a glass chapel at a Paris Salon in the autumn of 1930 and these subjects probably date around that time; indeed one crucifix was made for that chapel. In 1933 Lalique exhibited a larger chapel.

Opposite, Statuette "Suzanne." Molded nude with drapery. "R. Lalique," molded signature. Engraved signature on base "R. Lalique France" No. 833. c.1930. (Sotheby's Belgravia Sale. August 3, 1971.)

Surtout or centerpiece, "Deux Cavaliers." Molded panel with frosted intaglio of
two horsemen on web-footed horses, joisting. Bronze base with pattern of cobwebs
and stems, mounted for electricity. Glass engraved "R. Lalique." c.1930.
(Sotheby's Belgravia Sale, March 28, 1973.)

Statuette "Grande Nue." Molded nude
with base of ivy design on stand of
carved wood. Glass engraved "Lalique."
Before 1932. (John Jesse Gallery.)

Decorative motif, two swallows on glass base.
Clear pressed glass. Height, 14¼ inches.
"R. Lalique" in block letters. c.1926-1932.
(The Toledo Museum of Art.)

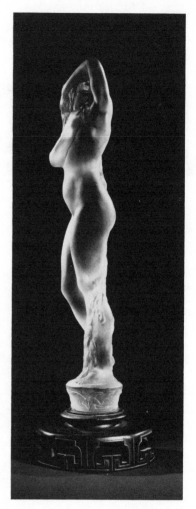

Crucifix. Frosted glass; figure in relief against black cross. Height with base 13 inches, width 6½ inches. Lalique, c.1930. (The Toledo Museum of Art.)

Sitting cat, 8¼ inches high. Two sparrows, c.4¼ inches long. Luminous satin finish. Lalique, c.1930 to present.

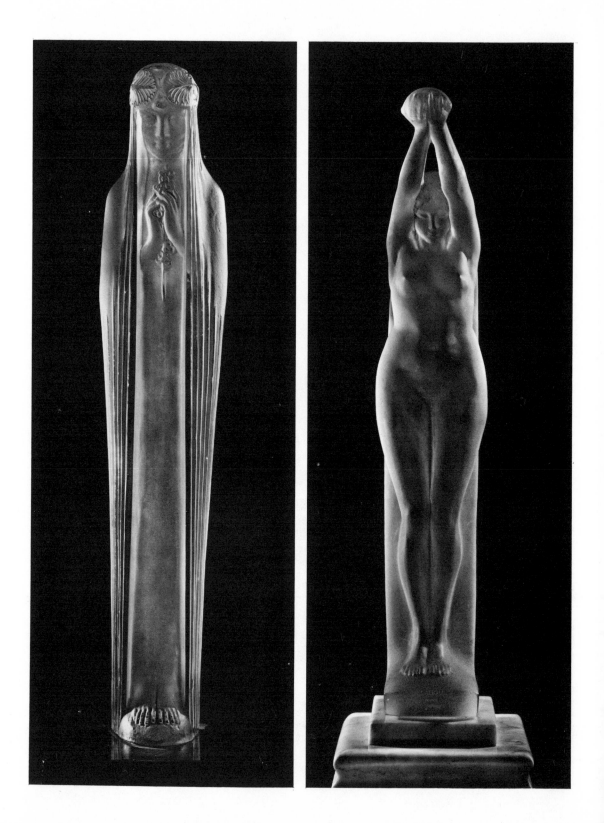

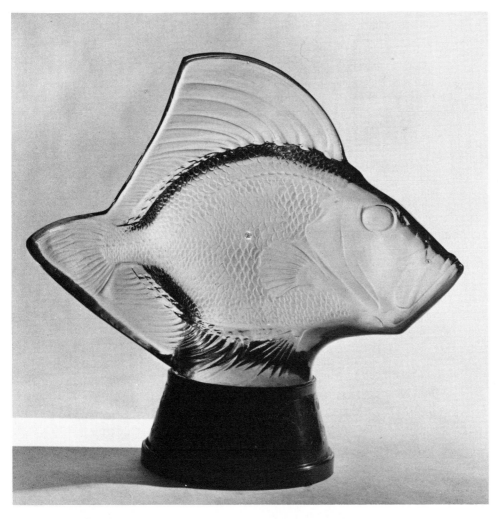

Gros Poisson Vagues, No. 1100. Light on bronze stand mounted for electricity.
Colorless glass. "R. Lalique." (Sybarites Gallery Inc.)

Opposite, left: Statuette, "Source de la Fontaine," No. 837. Colorless glass on
wooden stand. Figure with flower in hands. No. 700. "R. Lalique."
Before 1932. (Sybarites Gallery Inc.)

Opposite, right: Statuette "Grand Nue," arms raised. No. 835. Frosted
colorless glass. Mark, "R. Lalique France" in block letters. (Sybarites
Gallery Inc.)

"Grand Nue" with long hair on base
with ivy relief set on carved wooden
stand. R. Lalique before 1932.
(Editions Graphiques Ltd.)

Figure experimental, *cire perdue*.
"R. Lalique" in scratched block letters.

"Tête Penchée." Veiled figure in relief on oval with border of blossoms. Made in both clear crystal and color. Height, c.15 inches. Signed "R. Lalique." Before 1932. (Courtesy Fred Silberman, Antiques Center of America.)

❧❧ CLOCKS, MIRRORS, AND PICTURE FRAMES

Clocks have been an important decorative accessory since their invention. Although a timepiece of some sort dates back many centuries, the clock as we know it did not come into existence until the Middle Ages. French clocks of the periods of Louis XV and Louis XVI were works of art combining marquetry of precious woods, bronze and gilt mountings, and valuable jewels. In conjunction with other decorative accessories the clock was harmonious with the design and color of the furniture and other articles in a room.

The clocks of Lalique were no exception to the rule. In line, form, color, and motifs of design Lalique clocks were in harmony with the decorative surroundings of the 1920s and 1930s. Birds, butterflies, flowers, and nudes or veiled figures conform to the graceful designs of the period rather than to the later modernistic Cubist trends.

Lalique invented lighting fixtures and clocks made of sheets of glass about an inch in thickness with a design deeply etched by acid on the back of the glass. These clocks were mounted on a base which held a concealed electric bulb and the light from the bulb shone up through the thickness of the glass illuminating the incised design. This technique was used in a circular clock with two nude figures of a man and a woman surrounding the clock face. The male figure was cut in intaglio, the female in cameo and the different treatment gave a contrast of dark and light when the light in the bronze base was switched on. This important clock was called "Le Jour et la Nuit." It was first made in the 1920s. There were 3,500 copies of this clock available in *blanc* crystal in 1932. "2 Figurines" was the name of a clock with arched top with a molded figure of a woman in Grecian costume on either side of the dial which was wreathed in flowers. This clock was also first made in the 1920s. Another popular clock was called "2 Colombes." There were two figures of doves sitting in the arched space above the clock dial; 1,350 were available in *blanc* and 1,500 in *couleur* in 1932. "Sirènes" was a square clock with molded figures of nudes and ropes of pearls; 2,200 were available in *blanc* and 2,500 in *couleur* in 1932. Another large clock "Feuilles" had a design of molded leaves about the circular clock case. There were 950 of this model available in *blanc* and 1,100 in *couleur* in 1932.

All of these above mentioned clocks were wired for electricity and were probably the most important clocks made by Lalique.

There was also a group of small eight-day clocks made in *blanc* crystal with molded designs on the clock case. These, as listed in the 1932 Lalique Catalogue, were:

No. 731   "Roitelets" (wrens) *Blanc* 1,125.

No. 732   "Papillons" (a round glass case engraved with butterflies) *Blanc* 1,175.

No. 733   "Muguet" (a round glass case engraved with a wheel-like border of lily of the valley) *Blanc* 1,175.

No. 734   "Marly" (a small circular clock case with sprays of lily of the valley accented with enamel, *Blanc* 1,075.

No. 735   "Rossignols" (a round glass clock case on a glass base with each hour on the clock face marked with a figure of a nightingale) *Blanc* 1,100.

No. 736   "Hélène" (a rectangular clock case ornamented with flower garlands and three nude figures on the pediment) *Blanc* 1,000.

There was also a group of small eight-day clocks listed as "Pendulettes" with square or rectangular cases. These included:

No. 760   "4 Perruches" (four parakeets on blossoming branches on either side of the clock face) *Blanc* 700.

No. 761   "5 Hirondelles" (five flying swallows grouped about the face of a small upright rectangular clock) *Blanc* 700.

No. 763   "6 Hirondelles" (a design of six swallows sitting on tree branches about the face of an upright rectangular clock) *Blanc* 700.

No. 762   "Marguerites" (a clock decorated with a molded pattern of marguerites about the rectangular clock case) *Blanc* 700.

No. 764   "Naïades" (a small square clock case decorated with figures of nude water nymphs with flowing pearly hair) 550 in pale opalescent color.

No. 765   "Inséparables" (a small square clock with birds grouped on branches on either side of the clock face) 550 in pale opalescent glass.

No. 766   "Pierrots" (a tiny round clock with frosted figures of two birds at the top center) *Blanc* 500.

No. 767   "Antoinette" (a small round clock with frosted figures of two birds at top center) *Blanc* 850.

Hand mirrors were among some of the early articles made by Lalique at the end of the 1890s when he was still designing jewelry. There was a mirror with a frame of serpent design and a mirror with a plaquette containing a figure of Narcissus and a border ornamentation of narcissus blossoms. It was called "Narcisse Couché." This mirror was made for many years and was included in the 1932 Catalogue which lists 800 in clear and frosted glass. There were also small oval mirrors made to hang on cords or chains and probably to carry in a purse. The backs of these little mirrors had relief designs of the following: "Psyché," a nude figure with wings; a figure of Narcissus standing; an Art Deco design of a locust; a design called "Tête." All of these designs were made in *blanc* or colorless glass.

A group of larger round mirrors were made with handles or decorative silk tassels. The designs included: "Oiseaux" (birds); "Chèvres" (goats); "Muguets" (lily of the valley); "3 Paons" (peacocks). All were made in large quantities in *blanc* or colorless glass. The 1932 Catalogue also illustrates two large round mirrors, "Rond Grand Eglantine," a design of wild roses and "Rond Grand Epines," a design of hawthorn. Each design is divided into panels and separated by bands of cords or ribbon all executed in relief on colorless glass. These were made in quantities of thousands, so there should be some available to the collector. A large mirror was also made with a frame of serpents.

Lalique also put many of his popular designs on picture frames. There were square, rectangular, and round picture frames with relief decoration made in several sizes and in both color and colorless glass. The designs included the "Inséparables" (parakeets on blossoming branches) which was available in both colored and colorless glass. A small square frame was ornamented with a design of "Muguets" (lily of the valley) and the well-known design "Naïades" (nudes with long pearly tresses) was on another small picture frame. "Guirlandes" was the name of a design of daisies and *bergeronettes* or wag-tail birds nested in the foliage of the engraved design of that name on another frame. Other patterns included: "Hirondelles" (swallows); "Etoiles," a design of stars; "Lys" (lilies); "Bleuets," an allover pattern of these flowers; "2 Figurines et Fleurs," a small round frame with a design of nudes and flowers and an oval center mirror. A large frame "Laurea Grand Modèle" was an Art Deco design of interlacing borders engraved with zig-zag patterns. All of these frames were made in both *blanc* and *couleur*.

The collector may not want to concentrate on mirrors and picture frames, in fact there are not too many available, but the designs include several that are not found on other articles of Lalique glass. Mirrors and *cadres*, or picture frames, listed in the 1932 Catalogue are as follows:

MIRRORS

No.	675	Miroir "Narcisse couché" (hand mirror) *Blanc* 800.
No.	677	Miroir rond "2 Oiseaux" *Blanc* 500.
No.	678	Miroir rond "2 Chèvres" *Blanc* 500.
No.	679	Miroir rond "3 Paons" gland (tassel de soie) *Blanc* 650.
No.	680	Miroir ovale "Sauterelles" (grasshopper) *Blanc* 250.
No.	681	Miroir ovale "Psyché" *Blanc* 250.

No. 682   Miroir ovale "Tête" *Blanc* 250.
No. 683   Miroir ovale "Narcisse debout" (standing) *Blanc* 250.
No. 684   Miroir rond "Muguets" gland de soie. *Blanc* 550.
No. 685   Miroir rond grand "Eglantines" *Blanc* 2,800.
No. 686   Miroir rond grand "Epines" *Blanc* 2,800.

All round mirrors are large, 160 mm. Oval mirrors are small, 70 mm., and "rond grand" mirrors are 430 mm. Mirrors were made in *blanc* or clear glass.

CADRES OR PICTURE FRAMES

No. 250   Cadre "2 Figurines et fleurs" *Blanc* 600.
No. 253   Cadre "Muguets" (lily of the valley) *Blanc* 225, *couleur* 250.
No. 254   Cadre "Bleuets" *Blanc* 600.
No. 255   Cadre "Laurea" (pattern of interlacing lines) *Blanc* 650.
No. 256   Cadre "Bergeronnettes" (birds and fruit) *Blanc* 375, *couleur* 425.
No. 257   Cadre "Hirondelles" (swallows with spread wings) *Blanc* 275, *couleur* 325.
No. 258   Cadre "Inséparables" (pairs of love birds in branches) *Blanc* 250, *couleur* 300.
No. 259   Cadre "Etoiles" (pattern of stars) *Blanc* 450, *couleur* 550.
No. 260   Cadre "Lys" (pattern of lilies in relief) *Blanc* 600, *couleur* 725.
No. 263   Cadre "Guirlandes" (pattern of flower garlands) *Blanc* 225, *couleur* 250.
No. 264   Cadres "Naïades" (nudes with flowing pearly hair) *Blanc* 300.

Opposite:
Above, Clock of clear opaline glass with figures of love-birds in relief and painting of same birds on clock dial. "Inséparables." No. 765. Signed "R. Lalique" in glass. (Christie sale, December, 1973.)

Below, Clock "Le Jour et la Nuit." Intaglio and cameo technique on glass stand. No. 728. *Couleur*, 3500. Before 1932.

Silver hand mirrors. *Left*: Leaf and vine design. *Right*: Art Nouveau design of figures and leaf scrolls. R. Lalique, c. 1917. (Editions Graphiques Ltd.)

Opposite:

Above left, Clock "Two Figurines," molded glass ornamentation. No. 726. Lalique c.1926. 3500 available in *couleur* in 1932.

Above right, Small 8 day clock. No. 761. Lalique. 700 available in "blanc" in 1962.

Below, Mirror, molded colorless glass. Lalique. c. 1930-1940. (Martin Cohen.)

89

❧ ❧ PERFUME BOTTLES

Perfumes and essences were known in ancient Egypt and early Greece. The first perfume containers were terra cotta with grotesque head stoppers. There were also bottles of carved onyx and alabaster. The eighteenth century was the real beginning of the perfume industry. In France, Revillon, Houbigant, and Lubin were all established as perfumers at this time. The French perfume containers were flacons with straight sides and molded designs in the style of Louis XV or enameled with flowers or Watteau figures. This was the period when exquisite articles *de toilette* came into use. There were flacons of cut crystal, Sèvres, and Meissen porcelain, and of painted enamel with mountings of engraved gold or ornamented with wood marquetry. There were also bottles of Battersea enamel and Chelsea bottles in the form of animals, Chinamen, and dancing figurines. Bottles of opaline glass were decorated with flowers and butterflies. In England, Apsley Pellat (c. 1820) made cut glass bottles with cameo portrait medallions of Royalty and other famous people. Tiny blown glass Nailsea perfume bottles with fluted necks, dates, and inscriptions were sold at fairs for almost nothing but they have become valuable collectors' items today.

By the nineteenth century the fine perfumers realized the need of special packaging for their perfumes and for the collector of glass perfume bottles this is the important period. The manufactory of Baccarat was founded in 1764. In the mid-nineteenth century the square or round cut glass flacons with decorative designs and hermetically sealed stoppers made by Baccarat were an elegancy of supreme distinction in the Second Empire. Other glass houses besides Baccarat that were making perfume bottles at this time were Cristalleries de Nancy, Cristalleries de Saint Louis, Verreries d'Argenteuil, Viard, and Viollet-le-Duc. In the 1880s cut glass bottles were made in contrasting colors heavily engraved at Stourbridge in England.

At the end of the nineteenth century the genius glassmaker Emile Gallé often created flacons of cameo glass. However the flacons of Gallé were never made for commercial distribution but created as unique pieces to be placed in a vitrine for display.

Lalique too had been experimenting with glass since the 1890s and some of his earliest pieces were small perfume flacons. There was one in Egyptian design and another with a serpent motif. In 1902 Lalique employed four workmen in a glass studio at Clairfontaine, but it was not until 1907 that he exhibited perfume flacons in the vitrines of his shop in the Place Vendôme. M. François Coty had been packaging his perfume in bottles made by Baccarat but when he saw the Lalique flacons Coty approached Lalique with the project of designing for Coty perfumes. The bottles which were made in mass production were manufactured by Legras & Cie. de St. Denis. The flacons were of artistic and harmonious design adapted to the particular essence. Some of the bottles were in Art Nouveau design. This collaboration revolutionized the perfume industry and from this time on all perfumers used decorative bottles for packaging their perfumes.

Although the Coty records are not too clear as to which was the first bottle made by Lalique for Coty, one of the earliest bottles was made for the scent "Ambre Antique" in 1910. Under the heading "Lalique Series" the Coty catalogue of 1928 lists the perfums "Le Cyclamen," "Ambre Antique," and "Styx" with illustrations of the bottles designed by Lalique. In the 1937 Coty catalogue the "Ambre Antique" and "Styx" Lalique bottles are illustrated. The bottle which Lalique designed for "Ambre Antique" followed the Mediterranean concept and was a graceful slender shape of amber glass ornament with figures of women in Grecian costume. The bottle was stamped "R.Lalique" in block letters. A tall slender bottle etched with nude figures and a rounded flat stopper marked "Cyclamen" was designed for "Le Cyclamen" perfume. The perfume "Styx" was also presented in 1910. The bottle was of cut crystal with a molded stopper. There are several sizes and styles of paneled bottles with decorative stoppers that were made for "Styx." The Lalique bottle for "L'Effleurt" depicts a nude dancing figure in a panel among flowers of Art Nouveau style and the stopper is a geometric design enameled in black. It is marked "Lalique L'Effleurt De Coty." A squat circular bottle is marked "Au Coeur des Calices Coty." It has a stopper with a decorative pressed design and is illustrated in a Lalique catalogue. There were other interesting bottles made for Coty perfumes but the records do not tell whether they were made by Lalique or not. The perfume "Jacée" in a square cut crystal bottle with carved stopper packaged in a box of Chinese design is illustrated in the 1937 Coty catalogue. The bottle for "Heliotrope" has a decorative molded stopper and the bottle for "Paris" (1922) is of pale blue glass in a flattened circular form with molded floral stopper and a case decorated with a view of Paris on a blue ground. The bottle for "A Suma" (1929) was round with a molded floral pattern. It was boxed in a lacquer-red box decorated with Oriental motifs. Both this box and the autumn leaf box which was used for "Jacée," "L'Ambre Antique," "L'Emeraude," and "L'Origan" may have been designed by Lalique because we do know that he designed the well-known powder box for "L'Origan" which is still in use. The perfume "Le Vertige" (1936), probably the last fragrance created by M. Coty before his death, was packaged in a bottle with molded design but the records do not indicate if it was of Lalique glass.

Two interesting perfume bottles were illustrated in a Lalique catalogue: No. 528 "Flacon Satyre" has a molded satyr head in the bottle extending from the end of the stopper; No. 528 "Jeunesse" has a molded figure of a nude cherub at the end of the stopper which extends down into the bottle. Both of these flacons are rare.

Lalique also designed bottles for other French perfume manufacturers including D'Orsay, Roger et Gallet, Arys, Rigaud, Forvil, Vigny, and Worth between 1910 and 1925. For Forvil he designed the bottle for "Perle Noire" and for Worth Lalique designed the bottle for "Je Reviens," "L'Ambre" for Vigny and "Les Deux Colombes" for D'Orsay. These included tall mushroom-stoppered bottles, round bottles decorated with mollusks of contrasting colors, and engraved bottles of mushroom or sea urchin shape made for Worth. The bottles were of clear crystal with moldings, sunken panels, and decorative stoppers. If color was used it was pale mauve, blue, green, antique ivory, amber or topaz to harmonize with the amber, topaz and emerald of the essences. There were a variety of forms—flat, round, cylindrical, cubic, oval, and stirrup-cup shapes. Some bottles had long silk tassels attached to their neck. The designs drew inspiration from the Orient, from classic Greece and Rome, and from French historic styles, as well as from new motifs of Art Deco. There were bottles with dancing nudes and garlands of flowers on a diadem stopper for "Leurs Ames D'Orsay." A bottle for D'Orsay perfume, c. 1912, has tall figures of Grecian women set in panels. Another bottle for D'Orsay perfume was of oval form molded with an allover pattern of lines and had a tall Grecian figure for a stopper. Bottles for Arys were of plain oval or round shapes with decorative stoppers. The bottles for La Parfumerie Rigaud were ornamented with molded designs and had large decorative stoppers. Several strikingly designed bottles were made for Roger et Gallet perfumes. One oval bottle had a sunburst flower design and the bottle for "Paquert" had an elaborate circular stopper with engraved daisies which enclosed the top of the bottle in a grand floral diadem similar to those of Lalique lights. The green bottle for Roger et Gallet "La Jade" has a design of tropical birds in relief. Within ten years Lalique is known to have manufactured from 250 to 500 million perfume bottles for various French perfumers.

In about 1909 Lalique opened Verrerie de Combs-la-Ville where he manufactured his own glass on a commercial scale. This glass included vases, statuettes, perfume flacons, and many other articles with molded, engraved, and enameled designs.

The perfume bottle had been such a success that Lalique continued to include flacons, *brûle-parfums*, and *garniture de toilette* in many different designs in his commercial output of glass from about 1909 until the present day. The 1932 Lalique Catalogue lists between 90 and 100 different designs of perfume bottles with three plates illustrating the designs. Many of the flacons illustrated were first made as early as 1912; some are made in clear crystal, others are also made in color, and still others are decorated with enamel. There are a few flacons with decorative tiara stoppers that are especially valuable collector's items. As listed in 1932 Catalogue they include:

No. 493   "Bouchon Fleurs de Pommier" (bottle with an allover design of scallops and tiara-type bouchon or stopper of engraved apple blossoms) 500 were available in clear transparent glass.

No. 494   "Bouchon Cassis" (plain paneled bottle with a tiara stopper of grapes) 225 were listed in clear glass, 250 in color.

No. 495   "Bouchon Mûres" (rectangular paneled bottle with a tiara stopper of mulberries) 225 were listed in clear glass, 250 in color.

No. 496   "Bouchon 3 Hirondelles" (plain bottle with a tiara stopper of three flying swallows) 250 were available in clear transparent glass.

No. 507   "Bouchon Eucalyptus" (slender bottle with a tiara stopper of eucalyptus pods and leaves) 130 were available in clear glass, 165 in color in 1932.

No. 525   "Muguet" (small flacon with a bunch of lily of the valley as a stopper) 125 were available in clear glass.

No. 526   "Clairfontaine" (small round bottle with a spray of lily of the valley on the stopper) 150 available in clear glass. Still being produced.

Other especially interesting perfume flacons are:

No. 514   "Amphridite" (engraved and molded bottle in the shape of a snail shell with the kneeling figure of a nude as a stopper) 115 were listed in clear glass, 140 in color in 1932.

No. 524   "Tantôt" (tall oval bottle with a molded design of fan-like leaves and a molded stopper of the same design) The bottle was first made in 1924. In the 1932 catalogue 80 are listed in clear glass, 100 in color.

No. 502   "Serpent" (An oval flacon molded in a pattern of a serpent's skin with a stopper in the form of a molded serpent) In 1932 only 50 were available in clear glass. This bottle is also found with an engraved serpent.

No. 508   "Telline" (small bottle in the shape of a clam shell molded with a pattern of the shell and with a stopper in the form of a shell) It was available in small quantity: 65 in clear glass, 80 in color.

No. 475   "4 Cigales" (tall rectangular bottle with four molded cicada) First made c. 1912. In the 1932 Catalogue 185 were listed in clear glass, 200 in color.

No. 477   "A Côtes Bouchon Papillon" (rounded squat bottle with molded butterflies on the stopper) 100 were available in clear glass in 1932.

No. 490   "Méplat, 2 Figurines" (flattened rectangular bottle with an oval panel of two nude figurines and a stopper with molded figurines) 450 were listed in clear glass.

No. 489   "Fougères" (tiny rectangular bottle with a molded pattern of ferns and an oval medallion of the bust of a woman with a mirror) There were 350 listed in clear glass.

No. 488   "Rosace Figurines" (round bottle with a design of nude figurines and fan-like molded stopper) First made in the 1920s. 250 were listed in clear glass in 1932.

No. 476   "Pavot" (small rounded bottle molded with a design of the petals of a poppy) It has a decorative molded stopper. First made in the 1920 s. In 1932, 150 were available in clear glass.

No. 522   "Hélène" or "Lotus" (a small squat bottle molded with a pattern of lotus leaves and seed pods) In 1932, 70 were available in clear glass and 80 in color.

Nos. 511 –512   "2 Danseuses" "6 Danseuses" (two flattened round bottles with designs of nude dancers) There were 350 of each bottle available in clear glass.

No. 487   "Panier de Roses"—one of the loveliest bottles—a tall column with a pattern of trellis work over the bottle engraved with roses. A molded border of roses at the top of the vase and a stopper of molded roses. Only available in clear glass.

No. 484   "Capricorne"—also an interesting bottle—has an engraved and enameled design of scarabs on the bottle and on the flattened round stopper.

No. 504   "Pan" (bottle with a masque of the god Pan and garlands of leafy ornament) Made in clear glass. Only 80 were listed in 1932.

There were several bottles with molded handles and stoppers and some of the leaf patterns that were used on large vases were also to be found on the bottles. No. 519, "Cactus," a frosted bottle with enameled pattern of all-over dots is still being made.

The 1932 Catalogue also illustrates several larger bottles for brûle-parfums. The molded designs on these bottles are particularly interesting. "Sirènes" is a bottle with molded figures of nudes. "Papillons" has a molded pattern of butterflies. "Faune" is a cylinder-shaped bottle with a pattern of fluting and circles and a stopper in the shape of a nude figure. Brûle parfum "Carrousel" is a round bottle with frosted figures of birds. These are all desirable bottles.

Flacons were also included in the *garniture de toilette* sets for a lady's dressing table. The "Enfants" pattern had a band of molded nude infants. This set included a round box and a vaporizor and was made in both clear and colored glass. Another pattern of garniture de toilette was "Perles," a design of ropes of pearls which included bottles of three sizes, covered boxes, and trays and was made in both polished and satin glass. "Epines," a pattern of molded hawthorn included bottles of four sizes, boxes of three sizes, and trays for hairpins, combs, and soap. It was made in both clear and enameled

Opposite: left, Perfume flacon "Capricorne." Engraved and lacquered design of beetle on clear crystal. Marked, "R. Lalique" in rounded script. Before 1932.

Right, Perfume flacon "Panier de Roses." Molded and engraved design on clear crystal. Lalique, before 1932. (both, John Jesse Gallery.)

glass. The pattern "Fleurettes" had a narrow molded floral border at the edges and on the stoppers of bottles and boxes and on the rims of trays. There were three sizes of bottles, two covered powder boxes, three rectangular trays, and one oval bowl. The pattern was available in both transparent and satin glass. The pattern "Myosotis" was decorated with narrow borders of floral design and had a figurine stopper. There were three sizes of bottles and a round covered box. A garniture de toilette called "Duncan" had a center panel of molded nudes with molded line borders. There were three sizes of square bottles and two small vertical rectangular bottles, one a vaporizer. There was also a covered square box and a square tray, both with figure panels and two undecorated rectangular trays and a transparent undecorated round bowl. The attractive "Dahlia" pattern had a large molded flower on the sides of the bottles and vaporizers and the tops of two covered boxes. This pattern is still in production. In about 1950 Lalique made an apple-shaped bottle for the Nina Ricci "Fille d'Eve" perfume. Also today there are several Lalique bottles made for Nina Ricci perfumes. These include the heart-shaped bottle with molded floral design made for "Coeur-Joie" and the bottle and dusting powder box with stoppers of a gracefully sculptured single or double dove which is made for "L'Air du Temps." These bottles are collectors' items and the empty bottles often sell for more than the bottles when they were filled with perfume.

Above left, Perfume flacon, "Pan," with design of head of Pan and garlands in relief. Clear crystal. Lalique before 1932. (John Jesse Gallery.)

Above right, Perfume flacon "Serpent." Molded pattern of snake skin with serpent stopper. Clear crystal before 1932. (John Jesse Gallery.)

Left, Perfume flacon "Carré Hirondelles" with relief design of flying swallows. Clear crystal, Lalique, before 1932. (John Jesse Gallery.)

Above, Group of Lalique perfume flacons. Eagle seal at far right. (Sotheby Belgravia Sale, June 22, 1972.)

Right, Dusting powder box of frosted crystal with molded figure of dove. (Nina Ricci Parfums.)

Above left, Perfume bottle for "L'Effleurt de Coty." Relief panel of nude and molded stopper of Egyptian design tinted with black. Marked "R. Lalique." (Coty International.)

Above right, Perfume bottle for "Ambre Antique" with engraved classic figures and molded stopper. Marked "R. Lalique." c.1910. (Coty International.)

Right, Perfume bottle for "Cyclamen." Engraved with design of nudes. Lalique before 1928. (Coty International.)

Flacon with three groups of two nude dancers each in relief and figure of sitting
nude as stopper. R. Lalique, c.1925.

Group of perfume bottles. *Left*,
Lalique with molded butterfly stopper.
Rear center, Lalique with blossoms
in relief and flower stopper. *Front right*,
Lalique bottle with molded design of
artichoke leaves called "Marquita." All
before 1932. (Barry Friedman.)

Bottle with relief designs of nudes and
blossoms. (John Jesse Gallery.)

Brûle Parfum with Art Nouveau design of nude
sirens. R. Lalique, c.1920-1925. (Editions Graphiques
Ltd.)

ᔐ ᔑ DINNER SERVICES, CANDLESTICKS, AND ANNUAL PLATE

Lalique acquired his glassworks Verrerie d'Alsace René Lalique & Cie. at Wingen sur Moder in the Bas-Rhin, the historic glass making center of France, in 1920. At this time he enlarged his production of glass to include not only such articles as vases and statuettes, but also all sorts of useful pieces such as complete sets of services for the dining table. These table services included almost every article used on the dining table from hors d'oeuvre services to finger bowls. There were semicircular shaped side dishes, plates of several sizes, bowls, and sauce dishes, water glasses, goblets and glasses for different wines, champagne glasses, and champagne stirrers, ice buckets, saucers and cups with butterfly and flower handles, cheese dishes, sardine dishes with sardines in relief on their covers, knife rests, menus and holders for place cards. Carafes had matching glasses and services for port wine had matching trays and portable liquor cabinets consisted of a stand holding three liquor flacons. The service for orangeade consisted of a pitcher and matching glasses. There were also flower vases, figurines, plateaux for the center of the table—including the engraved "Cygnes" (swans)—candlesticks and candelabra. These articles were made in great quatities, the number varying with the popularity of the design. The patterns included Lalique's repertory of popular designs and the majority of the articles were made in both clear and colored glass.

Coupes and assiettes comprised the largest group and these were made in fifty different designs. The most popular design was "Coupe Sirènes" and in 1932 there were 2,200 bowls of this pattern available in colorless glass (*blanc*) and 2,500 in colored glass. "Martigues," a design of ten goldfish arranged on a bowl, was another favorite pattern. There were 900 available in *blanc* and 1,100 in colored glass. "Cyprins" was another plate with a fish design; 900 were available in colorless glass in 1932. The bowl "Phalènes" had a border of butteflies. This pattern was available in colored glass. "Flora Bella" a sunflower design; "Anvers," a pattern of seedpods, and "Anges," a stylized design of vase forms and leaves were also available in colored glass. There were 1,200 crystal bowls with figures of two mocking birds, "2 Moineaux Moqueurs," of frosted glass sitting on the rim of the bowl. Two unusual designs were "Madagascar," a bowl with heads of monkeys in relief and "Eléphants" a bowl with a wide flange and a band of elephants in frosted relief on the base of the bowl. Other attractive bowls included "Gazelles," a bowl with leaves and figures of gazelles, "Saint Vincent," a pattern of grapes and grape vines, and "Filix," a pattern of fern fronds. This last was available in color and colorless glass and also with the pattern outlined in enamel. It was made in both bowl and plate form. There were several patterns of allover designs of flowers and the bowl "Nemours" with a design of daisies in relief with enamel centers was made before 1932 and is still being produced. The bowl "Gui" (mistletoe) was made in several sizes. It sits on tripod glass feet and was made in *blanc, couleur,* and enameled glass.

Other attractive designs of bowls included "Coquilles," shells, made in both *blanc* and *couleur* and "Nonnettes," a pattern of birds available in color only. "Bol Fleur" was a small bowl in clear crystal accented with enamel. There were also bowls and plates in the "Ondines" pattern of nude sea maidens. Both bowls and plates were made in the popular "Calypso" design with figures of five watery nudes in relief. These were available in both colored and colorless glass. The plates were marked in their centers "R. Lalique" in block letters. There was also a small plate with a figurine and flowers. The plate was available in colorless glass. The pattern "Chasse Chiens" with a rim border of hounds chasing was made in clear crystal with accents of enamel. Other typical Lalique designs included "Véronique," "Volubilis," "Vernon" (daisy), "Chicorée," and "Eglantine." One of the most desirable bowls for the collector is "Armentières" which has a molded border of stylized roses around its rim. There were also several bowls with Art Deco designs.

The carafe was one of the most attractive pieces of Lalique tableware. Carafes were early in Lalique's glassmaking career at Verrerie de Combs-la-Ville. They were decorated with designs in relief and engraved and enameled designs. An interesting carafe is called "6 Figurines." It has alternating vertical panels of nudes in relief and clear glass. There was a goblet in matching design. This carafe is similar to the rare carafe in *verre blanc* which was exhibited in the Art Décoratif Salon in 1911. In addition to the panels of nudes the neck of the carafe is ornamented with "tears" of applied glass which terminate in frogs' heads. The carafe has a tall pointed stopper. This design relates to the earlier work of Lalique before he began mass production. The carafe is now in the Musée des Arts Décoratifs. It is marked "R.Lalique" in block letters at the base of a plain panel. The "Masque" carafe was also first made c. 1911. In the 1932 Lalique Catalogue it is listed as being available in color or enamel. The stopper was of molded glass but it was also available with a silver stopper. A vase of similar design with a masque medallion was also made. There is also a carafe with figures of two veiled dancing nudes. Another especially desirable design is "Carafe Coquilles." Its shape is that of a clam shell and it is pressed with the shell design and has a molded stopper of shell pattern. This carafe was made in both colored and colorless glass. An attractive design is a carafe with a thorny relief pattern and there is one with a hawthorn pattern in relief. Another desirable carafe is the one with molded square repeats ornamented with a zig-zag pattern. There is a carafe with a grape design and a slender carafe with tall pointed stopper with a design of marguerites. This has a goblet to match. A pyramid shaped carafe is also interesting.

Caves à liqueurs holding three flacons were made in large quantities of over 3,000 sets in colorless crystal. One set included a center flacon engraved with a figure of Pan and two side flacons with figures of Bacchantes. The "Cave Enfants" had stoppers of molded figures of infants. The bottles and rounded stoppers of "Cave Vigne" were decorated with an engraved design of vines. Another set of flacons had beaded borders and a stopper in the beaded pattern in relief.

Glasses and goblets were produced in a variety of shapes and designs. There were slender stemmed funnel-shaped glasses engraved with patterns of vines and convolvulus. There were also goblets with a frieze of molded personages, goblets with molded frogs at their bases, and others had a molded band of dogs, cocks, or lizards; still others had scenes of hunting dogs. These goblets were all available in color or enamel decoration. There were also goblets with engraved designs of spirals, a lotus, and poppy. *Services à porto* included a pitcher, tray, and matching glasses. The pitcher usually was ornamented with a molded design at its base and the glasses also had similar designs at their bases. The trays were ornamented with molded designs at their rims. "Bamboo" was an effective design of stepped borders of molded vertical bamboo stalks. There were also pitchers, glasses, and trays for services of orangeade and ice cream services consisting of a bowl and six dishes. These were made in a variety of designs in both colored and colorless glass. Round trays or *plateaux* were available in more than a dozen different patterns in both clear and colored glass.

There were vases especially made to hold flowers including vases of crystal with frosted molded figures of pigeons or crickets at the handles. A group of funnel-shaped vases had molded figures at their bases. These included figures of birds, cocks, flowers, or squirrels in frosted glass while the vase itself was in clear crystal with vertical fluting. The vase "Faune" had a base design of a faun's face in cut glass. Candlesticks were also made in designs to match these vases. The vase and candlestick "Mésanges" (tomtit) are still being made. There were many different designs of single candlesticks including birds, leaves, flowers, and geometric patterns. Two or three candlesticks were joined together to form candelabra. Especially effective was the design called "Volutes" which was of similar design to the vase made c. 1932. Another attractive candelabra had angled branches with sockets for four candles and was ornamented with a relief pattern of mountain ash leaves and berries. A *garniture de cheminée* consisted of a pair of three branched candelabra with frosted figures of flying wrens. There was a round clock with a frame of figures of the same birds and a funnel-shaped vase with wrens at the base also matched.

Dining tables of glass were also made by Lalique. These tables consisted of a sheet of transparent glass with an equally transparent base and had framework supports of chromium plated metal. The glass of these tables was ornamented with designs that were acid etched or made by sandblasting. The thick glass of the table top had an arrangement for lighting the central panel from underneath. The supports and glass plinth were cast. These tables were made in limited quantities. They were advertised by Breves Galleries, London, in *The Studio Yearbook* for 1931.

The following are lists taken from the 1932 Lalique Catalogue.

COUPES ET ASSIETTES (BOWLS AND PLATES)

No. 375   Coupe "Sirènes" (bowl with border of nudes) *Blanc* 2,200, *couleur* 2,500.

No. 376   Coupe trépied "Sirène" *Blanc* 800, *couleur* 925.

No. 377   Coupe "Martigues" (design of goldfish) *Blanc* 900, *couleur* 1,100.

No. 378   Coupe "Cyprins," plate (goldfish) *Couleur* 900.

No. 379   Coupe "Cyprins" refermée (bowl) *Couleur* 900.

No. 380   Coupe "Ondines" ouverte (nude) *Blanc* 185, *couleur* 200.

No. 381   Coupe "Ondines" fermée *Blanc* 185, *couleur* 200.

No. 382   Coupe "Lys" satiné tripod *Blanc* 160, *couleur* 200.

No. 383   Coupe "Volubilis" (design of leaves) *Blanc* 80, *couleur* 100.

No. 385   Coupe "Coquilles" (shells) *Blanc* 165, *couleur* 235.

No. 387   Coupe sur pied "Clairvaux" émail (bowl on stem with sculptured knob) *Blanc* 250, *couleur* 275.

No. 388   Coupe sur pied "Saint Denis" émail (bowl on stem with sculptured knob) *Blanc* 250, *couleur* 275.

No. 389   Coupe "Filix" (fern pattern) *Blanc* 160, *couleur* 250. Also with enamel)

No. 390   Coupe "Gazelles" (deer) *Blanc* 275, *couleur* 335.

No. 391   Coupe "Saint Vincent" (pattern of grapes and vines) *Blanc* 325, *couleur* 450.

No. 392   Coupe "Cernuschi" (deep bowl with rim of relief design) *Blanc 325, couleur 375.*

No. 393   Coupe "Armentières" (bowl with rim border of roses) *Blanc 375, couleur 425.*

No. 395   Coupe "Vernon" (three large flowers) *Couleur 65.*

No. 396   Coupe "Mont Doré" (wreath) *Couleur 100.*

No. 397   Coupe "Véronique" (three veronica blossoms) *Couleur 90.*

No. 398   Coupe "Nonnettes" (three groups of birds with spread wings) *Couleur 70.*

No. 399   Coupe "Montigny" (geometric design of lines) *Blanc 300, couleur 400.*

No. 400   Coupe "Crémieu" (geometric ropes and bubbles) *Blanc 250, couleur 350.*

No. 401   Coupe "Tournon" (flower heads) *Blanc 250, couleur, 300.*

No. 402   Coupe "Villeneuve" (star design in bowl) *Blanc 300, couleur 375.*

No. 403   Coupe "Madagascar" (border of monkey heads) *Blanc 375, couleur 500.*

No. 404   Coupe "Nemours" émail (allover pattern of flower heads with enamel centers) *Blanc 200, couleur 225.* (Still being made)

No. 405   Coupe "Fleurville" (consecutive borders of flower heads) *Blanc 160, couleur 225.*

No. 406   Coupe "Phalènes" (border of butterflies) *couleur 900.*

No. 407   Coupe "Flora Bella" (bursting blossoms) *Couleur 900.*

No. 408   Coupe "Anvers" (border and center of stems and seed pods) *Couleur 900.*

No. 409   Coupe "Rosace" (geometric pattern of borders of triangles) *Couleur 200.*

No. 410   Coupe "Anges" (pattern of angels and vases of flowers) *Couleur 900.*

No. 411   Coupe "Eléphants" (border of elephants in relief in base) *Blanc 800.*

No. 412   Coupe cristal "2 Moineaux Moqueurs" (mocking birds) *Blanc* 1,200.

No. 413   Coupe "Calypso" (nude sea maidens) *Blanc* 350, *couleur* 350.

No. 414   Assiette "Calypso" *Blanc* 400, *couleur* 400.

No. 414   Assiette "Eglantine" (crystal plate with group of flowers in relief in center) *Blanc* 210, *couleur* 210.

No. 3001   Assiette "Chasse Chiens" émail (plate with border of chasing hounds) *Blanc* 330.

No. 3002   Assiette "1 Figurine et fleurs" (nude figurine and flowers) *Blanc* 175.

No. 3003   Assiette "Ondines" (nudes) *Blanc* 225, *couleur* 260.

No. 3023   Assiette "Filix" (ferns) *Blanc* 350, *couleur* 375.

No. 3100   Coupe "Bol Fleur" émail (small bowl with large flower in relief) *Blanc* 140.

CAVES A LIQUEURS

No. 1184   Cave à liqueurs "Pan et Bacchantes"(carafes with figures of Pan and Bacchantes) *Blanc* 2,700.

No. 1185   Flacon seul "Pan." *Blanc* 300.

No. 1186   Flacon seul "Bacchantes." *Blanc* 300.

No. 1187   Cave à liqueurs "Enfant" (stoppers have pressed figures of infants) *Blanc* 2,250.

No. 1188   Flacon seul. *Blanc* 250.

No. 1189   Cave à liqueurs "Vigne" (design of vines) *Blanc* 2,250.

No. 1190   Flacon seul. *Blanc* 250.

No. 1201   Cave à liqueurs "Glasgow" (bottles with molded stoppers and edges) *Blanc* 2,250.

No. 1202   Flacon seul. *Blanc* 250.

BROCS ET CARAFES (PITCHERS AND CARAFES)

No. 3152   Carafe pyramidale (clear glass pyramid form) *Blanc* 150.

No. 3153   Carafe plate, "2 Danseuses" (carafe with center medallion of two dancers and garlands) *Blanc* 700.

No. 3155   Carafe "Reine Marguerite" (flowers) Enamel or *couleur* 450. Same vase with glass stopper, enamel or *couleur* 525.

No. 3156   Carafe "Masque" Enamel or *couleur* 450. Same carafe with glass stopper 525, with silver stopper 625.

No. 3157   Carafe "Aubépine" (hawthorn design) *Blanc* 525, *couleur* 600.

No. 3158   Carafe "6 Figurines" Enamel or *couleur*, 600. Goblet to match.

No. 3161   Carafe "Marguerites" bouchon pointu (marguerites with pointed stopper and goblet to match) *Blanc* 275, *couleur* 325.

No. 3163   Carafe "Coquilles" (clam shell design) *Blanc* 250, *couleur* 300.

No. 3164   Carafe "Vrilles de Vigne" (round form with design of vine tendrils) *Blanc* 200.

No. 3165   Carafe "Raisins" (grape design with glasses and tray to match) *Blanc* 225, *couleur* 275.

No. 3166   Carafe plate "Epines" (thorn design) *Blanc* 190, enamel or *couleur* 225.

No. 3169   Carafe "Dundee" (molded design or repeat squares with triangles) *Blanc* 175, enamel or *couleur* 200.

No. 3170   Carafe bantam. *Blanc* 100.

Today a new phase of collecting is centered on annual limited editions. This includes annual plates and other articles such as mugs, sculptures, paperweights, and commemorative medals of glass, porcelain, silver, or other metals which are sold as "limited editions." A limited edition is any object produced in multiples of a certain number after which the original mold or pattern is destroyed and production ceases.

Good antiques are getting more and more difficult to find and are now priced beyond the purse of the average collector. But the interest in collecting continues and limited editions provide a new field at a reasonable price and a continuing increase. In most cases prices have soared from year to year.

In 1965 René Lalique & Cie. of France decided to make an annual plate.

These plates are designed by Marie-Claude Lalique and grand-daughter of René Lalique. The subjects of the plates are drawn from nature but the motifs are stylized in a modern manner. The technique is a combination of transparent clear glass and satin etched surfaces. The first plate was issued in September 1965; 2,000 were made. This plate was a design of stylized flowers and branches and in the center of the plate are two decorative birds with necks entwined. The title of the plate is "Deux Oiseaux," two birds. The plates are 8½ inches in diameter. Each plate is dated and signed "Lalique France" in small script. This first plate was issued at $25 but now sells for about $2,000. The second Lalique plate was issued in May 1966. It is a design of a large single rose and is entitled "Dreamrose." A larger quantity (c. 3,000) of this plate was made. This plate now sells for about $500. The 1967 plate is a design of swirling seaweed and five fish. Issued at $25, the plate now sells for $400. The 1968 plate is a stylized deer with long curled horns; it now sells for $200. The 1969 plate is a modern design of a butterfly, star-like flowers, and stems; its present price is $150. A peacock was the inspiration for the 1970 plate. The peacock body is in the plate center and it is surrounded by conventionalized peacock feathers. The 1971 Lalique owl plate is the most dramatic design. Since owls are favorites with collectors the price should mount. In 1973 it was priced at $100. The 1972 Lalique plate has a large stylized shell. This plate which came out at $40 was priced at $75 in 1973. The 1973 Lalique plate is a large realistic eagle head; the eagle has long been a favorite Lalique motif. Between 8,000 and 10,000 plates are now made.

In collecting Lalique annual plates one should know how many plates there are in the edition. The name of the designer and the mark as well as the esthetic value are important. If you have lost out on the first plate pay a premium and buy it, as a complete collection has more value than single plates. The chance to collect an object that not everyone can have and the hope that it will increase at least to double or triple price not only as a collectable but as an investment is what lures the collector into the field.

Carafe with figures of nude maidens.
Applied glass ending in frogs' heads on
neck of carafe. Mark "R. Lalique" in
block letters near base. Before 1911.
(Musée des Arts Décoratifs.)

Glass bowl with design of whirling fish
and bubbles. Lalique before 1932.
(The Minneapolis Institute of Arts.)

LALIQUE GLASS
for the CONNOISSEUR

*Glass Table with design of
fruit and leaves — one of the
many exclusive exhibits at
Breves' Lalique Galleries.*

Among the works of René Lalique there are certain "collectors'
pieces" of such beauty and rarity that they are seldom to be
obtained outside Paris. The only exhibition in England which
includes these desirable acquisitions is at Breves' Lalique Galleries.
Not merely a small selection, but the
whole range of Lalique's creations is
here presented, and the prices are as
varied as the glass itself. Two books
of interest to every connoisseur of
glass – "The Art of René Lalique" and
"Lalique Lights" – will be sent post
free for 1s. 6d.

R. LALIQUE
France

A LALIQUE
FRANCE

R. Lalique France

*Every genuine example
of Lalique Glass bears
one of the artist's
marks reproduced here.*

BREVES' LALIQUE GALLERIES
2 BASIL ST., SLOANE STREET, LONDON, S.W.3
Lift to Galleries.
(Close to Knightsbridge Underground)   Telephone: Kensington 1928-7471

Advertisement of Breves' Lalique Galleries showing
glass table and Lalique marks. (Studio Yearbook,
1931.)

Right, Pair of candlesticks. Clear and frosted glass with molded leaf pattern partially polished. Height, 7⅞ inches. Mark "R. Lalique France" in block letters on base. (The Toledo Museum of Art.)

Below, Round platter, sculptured fern design radiating from the center. Diameter, 17½ inches. Signed "R. Lalique France" in block letters. (The Chrysler Museum at Norfolk.)

Lalique Annual Plate, 1968.
(Jacques Jugeat Inc.)

Below, Round plate, clear glass with
sculptured dandelion leaf design radiating
from center. Diameter 12 inches. Signed
"R. Lalique France." (The Chrysler
Museum at Norfolk.)

Lalique Annual Plate, 1969.
(Jacques Jugeat Inc.)

Shallow bowl fish pattern and
bubbles. Signed "Lalique" in
small script. Current production.
(Maler's Gift Gallery.) Orville
Voight, photo.

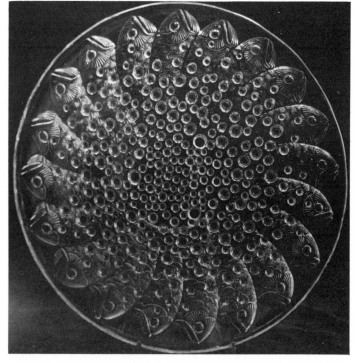

❧ ❧ RADIATOR CAPS
AND PAPERWEIGHTS

The first Lalique radiator caps were made in the middle or late 1920s. The "Archer," a design of a kneeling male nude with bow and arrow molded in intaglio was illustrated in *Mobilier et Décoration* in 1927; an article on Lalique radiator caps appeared in *The Studio* in 1931, and *The Studio Yearbook* for 1931 carried an illustration of the elongated racing greyhound that Lalique designed for H.R.H. Prince George. A similar design was later included in the 1932 Lalique Catalogue. These decorative *bouchons de radiateur* became so popular that forty-six designs were listed and illustrated in the 1932 Lalique Catalogue. The majority of the radiator caps were available in clear crystal (*blanc*) but some could also be had in *couleur*. Lalique's realistically modeled head of an eagle with molded feathers, part polished and part frosted, was used by officers of Hitler's Reich. This figure was 4½ inches in height and was marked "R.Lalique France" in block letters. According to the 1932 Lalique Catalogue there were 400 of these eagle heads available. The "Libellule" or dragonfly design was one of the most popular. It was made in two sizes: "Libellule Petite" with block letter signature and "Libellule Grande" which was 8½ inches in height and had an engraved and molded signature "R.Lalique France" in script. The dragonfly was fastened on a bronze base beneath which was attached a multicolored lighted disc connected to the dynamo of the car so that the disc revolved and cast rainbow shades of light through the insect which changed with the speed of the car. "Vitesse" a figure of a kneeling nude was also a popular model. It was available in both *blanc* and *couleur*. This figure was also made as a paperweight. A similar figure called "Danseuse" is now being manufactured. "Chrysis" was also a nude figure. Models of this figure were made in *blanc* and *couleur*.

A large figure of a cock, "Coq Houdan," was also a favorite radiator cap. It was available in both clear crystal and in color and was marked "R.Lalique France" in block letters. Other figures of cocks included "Coq Nain," a small figure in crystal and in color. A figure of five horses galloping in Greek style is 8½ inches in height. It was made in clear crystal and marked "R.Lalique" in block letters. "Epsom" and "Longchamps" were figures of horses' heads made in clear crystal. A woman's head "Victoire" or "Spirit of the Wind" with hair flying back in Art Deco style was first made before 1930. It was marked "R.Lalique France" and was listed as being made in clear crystal in the 1932 Lalique Catalogue. There was also a star in Art Deco style.

The complete list of radiator caps—Bouchons de Radiateur—as listed in the 1932 Catalogue is as follows:

BOUCHONS DE RADIATEUR

No. 1122   "5 Chevaux" (horses) *Blanc* 280.

No. 1123   "Comète (comet) *Blanc* 275.

No. 1124   "Faucon" (hawk) *Blanc* 285.

No. 1126   "Archer" (figure of nude archer engraved on circle of glass) *Blanc* 285.

No. 1135   "Coq Nain" (figure of small cock in clear and frosted glass) *Blanc* 400, *couleur* 435.

No. 1136   "Tête de Bélier" (head of ram) Marked "R.Lalique" in block letters. *Blanc* 285.

No. 1137   "Tête de Coq" (head of cock) *Blanc* 420.

No. 1138   "Tête d'Aigle" (head of eagle) *Blanc* 400.

No. 1139   "Tête d'Epervier" (head of hawk) *Blanc* 245, *couleur* 275.

No. 1140   "Tête de Paon" (head of peacock) *Blanc* 320, *couleur* 350.

No. 1141   "Lévrier" (greyhound) *Blanc* 285.

No. 1142   "Saint Christophe" (intaglio design of saint against a rayed figure of child on circle .of clear glass) Marked "R.Lalique France" in block letters. *Blanc* 285.

No. 1143   "Hirondelle" (figure of swallow with spread tail) *Blanc* 285.

No. 1144   "Petite Libellule" (small figure of dragonfly) *Blanc* 275.

No. 1145   "Grande Libellule" (large figure of dragonfly) *Blanc* 385.

No. 1146   "Grenouille" (small figure of frog) *Blanc 245, couleur 275.*

No. 1147   "Victoire" or "Spirit of Wind" (head of woman with stylized hair flowing out behind) *Blanc 450, c. 1930.*

No. 1152   "Longchamps" (head of horse) *Blanc 350.*

No. 1153   "Epsom" (straining head of horse) *Blanc 350.*

No. 1157   "Sanglier" (small figure of boar) *Blanc 245, couleur 275.*

No. 1158   "Perche" (figure of fish) *Blanc 295, couleur 320.*

No. 1160   "Vitesse" (speed, figure of kneeling nude with arms behind head) *Blanc 420, couleur 460.*

No. 1161   "Coq Houdan" (tall standing figure of cock) *Blanc 370, couleur 400.*

No. 1164   "Pintade" (figure of guinea fowl) *Blanc 295.*

No. 1181   "Hibou" (figure of owl) *Blanc 385.*

No. 1182   "Renard" (figure of running fox) *Blanc 635.*

No. 1183   "Chrysis" (figure of kneeling nude with arms stretched out back of head) *Blanc 460, couleur 485.*

Paperweights are also an interesting and less expensive item for the collector. Lalique made as many as fifty of these little figures. Some were the same designs as the radiator caps but there were also other figures such as the cat, the elephant, the rhinoceros, the bison, the horse, the moose, two turtle doves, and a double marguerite that were not made as radiator caps. However, according to the Catalogue any of the figures could be mounted as bouchons de radiateur at an extra cost of 135 francs. The majority of the paperweights are much smaller than the radiator caps.

The list of paperweights as given in the 1932 Lalique Catalogue is as follows:

PRESSE-PAPIERS (PAPERWEIGHTS)

No.   801   "2 Aigles" (two eagle heads) made in both *blanc 250, couleur 300.*

No. 802   "Double Marguerite" (sunburst design of marguerite) made in both *blanc* 225, and *couleur* 250.

Nos. 803 –04   "2 Sardines" and "3 Sardines" (small fish) available in *blanc*, 150 each.

No. 1126   "Archer" (figure of archer engraved on round disc of glass) 150 available in *blanc*.

No. 1128   "2 Tourterelles" (figures of two turtle doves with bills together) made in both *blanc* 400, and *couleur* 500, figures of doves frosted, floral base.

No. 1135   "Coq Nain" (small figure of cock) available in both *blanc* 265, and *couleur* 300.

No. 1136   "Tête de Bélier" (head of ram) signed "R. Lalique" in block letters. *Blanc* 150.

No. 1137   "Tête de Coq" (head of cock) *Blanc* 285.

No. 1138   "Tête d'Aigle" (eagle head) in clear and frosted glass.

No. 1139   "Tête d'Epervier" (head of sparrow hawk) in *blanc* 110 and *couleur* 140.

No. 1140   "Tête de Paon" (head of peacock with tall crest) *Blanc* 185 and *couleur* 215. Marked "R.Lalique" in block letters.

No. 1141   "Lévrier" (figure of greyhound engraved on plaque of glass) *Blanc* 150. Marked "R.Lalique" in block letters.

No. 1142   "Saint Christophe" (figure of St. Christopher against rayed background engraved on circular plaque of glass) Marked "R.Lalique France". *Blanc* 150.

No. 1143   "Hirondelle" (figure of swallow with spread tail) *Blanc*. Marked in block letters "R.Lalique France." *Blanc* 150.

No. 1145   "Libellule grande" (large figure of dragonfly) *Blanc* 250. Marked in script.

No. 1146   "Grenouille" (small figure of frog) *Blanc* 110 and *couleur* 140.

No. 1148   "Antilope" (small standing figure of antelope) *Blanc* 100 and *couleur* 125.

Nos. 1149   "Moineau Fier, Hardi, et Timide" (frosted figures of spar-
−1151   rows proud, bold, and timid) *Blanc* 125 each.

No. 1152   "Longchamps" (heads of horses) *Blanc* 215.

No. 1154   "Moineau sur socle, ailes croisées" (sparrow with wings crossed) *Blanc* 250.

No. 1155   "Moineau sur socle, ailes ouvertes" (sparrow on base with wings open) *Blanc* 250.

No. 1156   "Moineau sur socle, ailes fermées" (sparrow on base with wings closed) *Blanc* 250.

No. 1157   "Sanglier" (wild boar, frosted figure on stand) *Blanc* 110 and *couleur* 140. Still made in white frosted glass.

No. 1158   "Perche" (frosted and clear figure of perch) *Blanc* 160 and *couleur* 185.

No. 1159   "Cheval" (small figure of horse with arched neck) *Blanc* 100 and *couleur* 125.

No. 1161   "Coq Houdan" (large figure of standing cock) *Blanc* 235 and *couleur* 265.

No. 1162   "Chat" (reclining figure of cat on stand) *Blanc* 150 and *couleur* 175.

No. 1164   "Pintade" (figure of guinea fowl on stand) *Blanc* 160.

No. 1168   "Daim" (small figure of deer on stand) *Blanc* 110 and *couleur* 140. Still made.

No. 1176   "Barbillon" (small figure of barbel fish on base) *Blanc* frosted 135.

No. 1181   "Hibou" (figure of owl on round base) *Blanc* frosted 250.

No. 1182   "Renard" (large figure of fox standing on circular base) *Blanc* and frosted 500.

No. 1183   "Chrysis" (kneeling figure of nude with arms back of head) *Blanc* 325 and *couleur* 350.

No. 1191   "Eléphant" (elephant on rectangular stand with trunk thrown back) *Blanc* 600.

No. 1192   "Toby" (small figure of elephant standing on circular base) *Blanc* 125.

No. 1193   "Chouette" (small figure of barn owl) in satin finish. *Blanc* 100. Still made.

No. 1194   "Taureau" (satin finish bull on clear crystal base) Height 3½ inches. Signed in block letters on base "R.Lalique." *Blanc* 100. Still being made.

No. 1195   "Rhinocéros" (standing figure of rhinoceros) On rectangular clear crystal base. *Blanc* 150.

No. 1196   "Bison" (figure of bison with head down) On clear crystal rectangular base. *Blanc* 250.

No. 1197   "Renne" (small figure of moose standing on small rectangular crystal base.) *Blanc* 125.

Many of these paperweights are still being made. They are marked "Lalique" in block letters. The ones made in 1932 and before are marked "R.Lalique" in block letters.

Radiator cap, dragonfly. Height, 8½ inches. Engraved signature in script on side of body "R. Lalique France." 1925-1931. (Christie, photo A. C. Cooper.)

Radiator cap, "Petite Libellule," clear crystal. Signed on wing "R. Lalique France" in block letters. 1925-1931. (John Jesse Gallery)

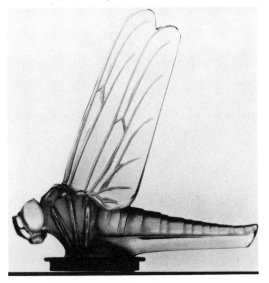

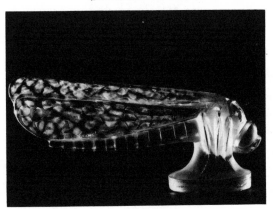

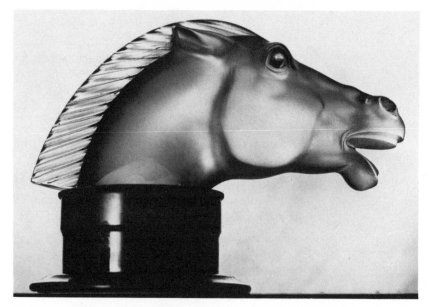

Radiator cap, horse's head "Epsom." c.1931. (John Jesse Gallery.)

Radiator cap, 5 horses. 8½ inches height. Marked "R. Lalique France" in block letters. 1925-1931. (John Jesse Gallery.)

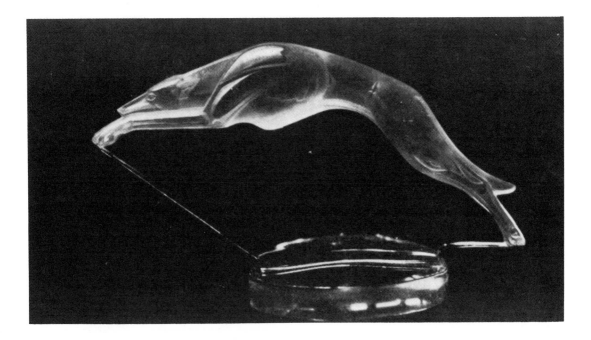

Above, Motor mascot designed for H.R.H. Prince George. c.1931. (Studio Yearbook, 1931.)

Left, Radiator cap "Hirondelle" (swallow) c.1931. (John Jesse Gallery.)

Right, Radiator cap, cock. Clear and
frosted glass. Height, 7⅝ inches. Marked
"R. Lalique France" in block letters.
c.1930 (The Toledo Museum of Art.)

Below, Radiator cap, Fish. Clear and
frosted glass. Height, 3⅞ inches. Marked
"R. Lalique France" in block letters.
c.1930.

Radiator cap, Archer. Intaglio on clear glass, figure frosted. Height, 5 inches. Marked "R. Lalique France." c.1930. (The Toledo Museum of Art.)

Radiator cap, Greyhound. Intaglio frosted figure in relief on clear glass.
Height, 3½ inches. Length, 7¼ inches. Marked "R. Lalique France" in block
letters. c.1930. (The Toledo Museum of Art.)

DESK FURNISHINGS: INKSTANDS, BLOTTERS, SEALS, AND ASHTRAYS

Between 1918 and 1922 Lalique had constructed a large factory at Wingen sur Moder in the Bas-Rhin especially planned for the mass production of objects in monotone pressed glass. The manufactory was called "Verrerie d'Alsace René Lalique & Cie." In addition to vases, lamps, statuettes, and other decorative objects that had been manufactured at Lalique's glassworks Verrerie de Combs-la-Ville since 1909 this new factory also manufactured many small household articles. The pieces included a large selection of useful and decorative articles such as complete sets of glass for a lady's dressing table; dining table services including plate, bowls, water and wine glasses, pitchers and carafes; furnishings for the writing desk. The first exhibition of this new collection of decorative accessories was in 1923. Among the quantities of small articles shown were fittings for the writing desk, including inkstands, seals, blotter covers, and ashtrays. These articles were manufactured in great numbers in a wide variety of designs and are evidence of the extensive commercialism that Lalique entered into in the 1920s and 1930s.

Inkstands were made in square and round shapes and in long rectangular forms which held two containers for ink and a trough for pens. There was also a rectangular glass tray or plateau that could be had with a figure of an eagle, pigeons, or mice. Small round ink bottles were made in the designs "Nénuphar" (water lily) in both *blanc* and *couleur*. A small round bottle called "3 Papillons" (butterflies) was a favorite, made in both *blanc* and *couleur*. Designs of other round bottles made in both *blanc* and *couleur* were "Mûres" (mulberries); "Serpents"; "Escargots" (snails); "Cernay," a leaf design; and "4 Sirènes," nude sea maidens, one of the most characteristic Lalique designs. The square bottle "Biches" was an Art Deco design of deer and greenery. It was an early bottle made in both *blanc* and *couleur* but continued to be made at least until 1932. The long rectangular inkstand called "Mirabeau" had a design of birds, fruit, and foliage. It was made with a sliding lid. "Sully" was a rectangular stand with a pattern of zig-zag borders and the long inkstand "Colbert" had a center container pressed with a design of leaves and berries.

Buvards or blotters were made in a group of interesting and characteristic Lalique designs. The designs included: "Grosses Feuilles" (large leaves); "Escargots" (snails); "Cerises" (cherries); "Faune et Nymphe" (deer and nude); "2 Sirènes enlacées, assises" (two sirens sitting in each other's arms); "Feuilles d'Artichauds" (artichoke leaves); "Mûres" (mulberries); and "2 Sirènes face à face couchées" (two sirens lying face to face). All of these blotter designs were in Art Nouveau style. Although one or two might not seem important a group could be framed or put under glass in a coffee table.

The small cachets or seals with decorative engraved or molded designs offer an inexpensive item for the collector of Lalique glass. There were about fifty different designs of Lalique seals. The majority of the seals were made in clear or frosted colorless crystal but some were also available in colored glass. Seals can be divided into two groups. There is one group of standing figures of animals and humans. The majority of the figures are animals including figures of dogs, rabbits, a fox, squirrels, mice, goats, and birds including the turkey, duck, pelican, eagle, pigeon, and sparrow; there were also designs of locusts and flies. Human figures included a group of four figures: a figure of a veiled nude, a figurine with clasped hands, and a small figure of "Victoire." The other group of seals included those of round or oval pieces of glass with engraved intaglio designs. The designs on these included swallows, flying storks, and the favorite "Perruches" or parakeets. There were also several designs of butterflies, coiled lizards, and one with the arms of England in relief. Flower designs included "Bleuets," "Fuchsias," "Double Marguerite," and "Vase Fleurs." There were three circles of glass with nude figures and flowers, and three ovals with the same designs that were used on jewelry pendants. These were a nude swinging on a flower garland, a winged nude, and "Sirènes." There were also round seals engraved with figures of a "Faune," a goat, and one of a chamois. One rectangular piece of glass has a relief design of athletes, and two figures of birds sit at the top of another rectangle of glass. An engraving of a ship, "Caravelle," is on another seal and the favorite "Naïade," a nude sea maiden with pearly tresses, decorated a rectangular piece of glass with curved top.

Seals could be engraved with a monogram of one, two, or three letters at a small extra cost; thus it is possible to find seals with various monograms as well as the Lalique mark. The new seals—like other pieces of new Lalique glass—are marked "Lalique France" in script.

Many of the seal designs were also used as center figures of ashtrays. These included the pelican, duck, two doves, sparrow, finch, turkey, dog, rabbit, squirrel, mouse, fox, and a standing figure called "Statuette de la Fontaine." Forty-four different designs are listed and illustrated in the 1932 Lalique Catalogue. The dish ashtrays were made of clear crystal with a sculptured figure of satin finish glass in the center. Others have a round, rectangular, or semicircular piece of glass with an engraved design in their centers. These panels were engraved with the following well-known Lalique motifs: "Naïade," a nude with flowing pearly tresses; "Caravelle," a galleon ship; "Faune," a figure of a man with cloven feet; "Bélier," a figure of a goat; "Athlètes," an upright rectangular panel with a band of athletes in relief; and "Chamois," a figure of a chamois engraved on a circular piece of crystal. The majority of these ashtrays were made in colored glass as well as clear crystal.

Round, oval, square, and star-shaped ashtrays were made with molded borders of floral, leaf, and nude designs. There is also a round ashtray with a border of beetles in relief and another with a border of birds in relief. A rare ashtray is molded with a dahlia design and has a figure of a butterfly sitting on its rim.

A group of small ashtrays with frosted figures in their centers that are the same designs as those made in 1932 and before are still available today. These are "Naïade," a figure of a sea maiden; "Caravelle," the engraved ship; "2 Colombes," two doves, the squirrel, the pelican, the mouse, the sparrow, and the finch. These are now marked "Lalique France" in script instead of the old mark "R.Lalique" engraved in block letters. There are two new attractive ashtray figures—a dolphin and two swans. The large masque that was made in bronze for the handles of the large spheroid vase "Masque" is now made in colored glass on a crystal ashtray.

Lalique used many of his popular figures as subjects for bookends. These included "Pintade" or guinea fowl, "Coq Houdan," "Coq Nain," and the horse's head, "Epsom." There were also bookends with the "Tête de Bélier" or ram's head and with figures of nude children. These were usually signed "R.Lalique France" in block letters.

The following is a complete list of seals made in 1932 and listed in the Catalogue of that year:

No. 175   Cachet "Tête d'Aigle" (head of eagle) *Blanc* 165, *couleur* 185.

No. 176   Cachet "4 Figurines" face (front) *Blanc* 100, angle (side) 100.

No. 178   Cachet rond "Bleuets"(round, kingfishers) *Blanc* 100, *couleur* 120.

No. 179   Cachet "Anneau, Lézards" (coiled lizards) *Blanc* 100.

No. 180   Cachet "Mouche" (fly) *Blanc* 175.

No. 181   Cachet "Statuette Drapée" (draped statuette) *Blanc* 175, *couleur* 190.

No. 182   Cachet "Poisson" (fish) *Blanc* 125, *couleur* 150.

No. 183   Cachet "Sauterelle" (grasshopper) *Blanc* 95, *couleur* 110.

No. 184   Cachet "Motif Aigle" (eagle stopper for inkwell) *Blanc* 325.

No. 185   Cachet "Motif Souris" (mouse stopper for inkwell) *Blanc* 325.

No. 186   Cachet "Motif Pigeons" (stopper for inkwell) *Blanc* 325.

No. 187   Cachet "Perruches" (parakeets) *Blanc* 185.

No. 188   Cachet "Hirondelles" (swallows) *Blanc* 185.

No. 189   Cachet "Vase de Fleurs" (vase of flowers) *Blanc* 185.

No. 190   Cachet "Papillon, ailes fermées" (butterfly, wings closed) *Blanc* 175.

No. 192   Cachet "Papillon, ailes ouvertes" (butterfly, wings open) *Blanc* 175.

No. 193   Cachet rond "Figurine dans les Fleurs" (figurine in flowers) *Blanc* 150.

No. 194   Cachet rond "2 Danseuses" (2 dancers) *Blanc* 150.

No. 195   Cachet "Armes d'Angleterre" (English coat of arms) *Blanc* 200.

No. 196   Cachet "Double Marguerite" *Blanc* 185, *couleur* 200.

No. 197   Cachet rond "3 Papillons" (3 butterflies) *Blanc* 150.

No. 198   Cachet rond "2 Perruches et Fleurs" (2 parakeets and flowers) *Blanc* 150.

No. 200   Cachet rond "2 Figurines et Fleurs" *Blanc* 200.

No. 201   Cachet ovale "Figurine Ailée" (figurine with wings) *Blanc* 200.

No. 202   Cachet ovale "Figurine" (balancing) *Blanc* 200.

No. 209   Cachet "Figurine, mains jointes" (figurine, hands joined) *Blanc* 175, *couleur* 190.

No. 210   Cachet "Victoire" (figure etched on glass) *Blanc* 65, *couleur* 75

No. 211   Cachet ovale "Sirènes" (nude female figures) *Blanc* 150.

No. 212   Cachet ovale "Fuchsias" (fuchsias) *Blanc* 150.

No. 213   Cachet rond "Cigognes" (storks) *Blanc* 150.

No. 214   Cachet "Lapin" (rabbit) *Blanc* 45, *couleur* 50.

No. 215   Cachet "Dindon" (turkey) *Blanc* 45, *couleur* 50.

No. 216   Cachet "Chien" (dog) *Blanc* 45, *couleur* 50.

No. 217   Cachet "Renard" (fox) *Blanc* 45, *couleur* 50.

No. 218   Cachet "Souris" (bat) *Blanc* 45, *couleur* 50.

No. 219   Cachet "Canard" (duck) *Blanc* 45, *couleur* 50.

No. 220   Cachet "Moineau" (sparrow) *Blanc* 45, *couleur* 50.

No. 221   Cachet "Naïade" (nude with flowing hair etched on glass plaque) *Blanc* 70, *couleur* 70.

No. 222   Cachet "Pélican" *Blanc* 45, *couleur* 45.

No. 223   Cachet "Pinson" (finch) *Blanc* 50, *couleur* 50.

No. 224   Cachet "Caravelle" (ship) *Blanc* 50, *couleur* 50.

No. 225   Cachet "Bélier" (goat) *Blanc* 50.

No. 226 Cachet "Chamois" *Blanc* 45.
No. 227 Cachet "Ecureuil" (squirrel) *Blanc* 80, *couleur* 80.
No. 228 Cachet "Faune" (faun) *Blanc* 60.
No. 229 Cachet "Athlètes" (moulded band of athletes on rectangular piece of glass) *Blanc* 550.
No. 230 Cachet "2 Colombes" (doves) *Blanc* 60, *couleur* 60.
No. 231 Cachet "Nice" (figures of two doves at top of rectangular piece of glass) *Blanc* 125.

Inkstand "Biches" with relief pattern of foliage and deer. Made in both clear and colored glass. c.1910. (Musée des Arts Décoratifs.)

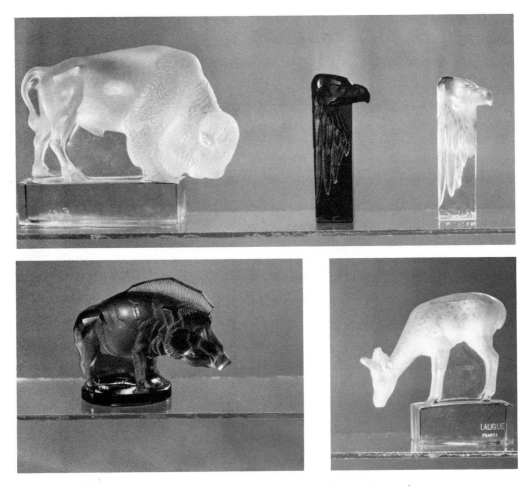

Seals. *Left to right*: Buffalo in frosted glass on clear base. Height, 3 13/16 inches.
c.1932-1940. Seal Hawk's head, black glass. Height, 3 3/16 inches. Signed in script,
"R. Lalique France." Same seal in clear and frosted glass. (The Toledo Museum of Art.)

Bottom. Figure of boar, dark grey glass frosted and clear. Height, 2 9/16 inches. c.1945.
(The Toledo Museum of Art.)   Seal, figure of deer. Frosted glass on clear base. Height,
3 3/16 inches. Marked "Lalique France." After 1945. (The Toledo Museum of Art.)

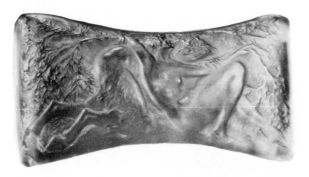

Buvard or blotter cover. "Faune et Nymphe." Blanc crystal. Marked "R. Lalique" in block letters, "France" in script. (Minna Rosenblatt.)

Buvard or blotter cover, Relief design of two nude sirens. Lalique. Before 1932. (Editions Graphiques Ltd.)

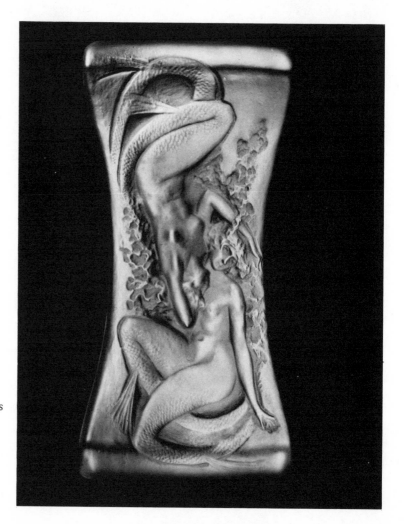

BOXES AND BONBONNIERES

Lalique made a great quantity of covered boxes. There were square and rectangular boxes for cigars and cigarettes and round sweetmeat boxes of various sizes, as well as several egg-shaped boxes. The box covers were molded with characteristic Lalique bird, flower, insect, and nude figure designs. The favorite peacock, dragonfly, cicada, sparrow, and wren designs seen on vases, clocks, and decorative motifs were also adapted to the tops of boxes. According to the number of boxes recorded in the 1932 Lalique Catalogue there should be many boxes available to the present day collector. However, while there are quantities of vases in the antique shops there seem to be few boxes. The "Houppes" or powder puff box design first made for Coty powder in 1913 was also available in glass of pale colors and opalescent glass. A box called "Roger" had a design of crystal cabochon circles on a background of birds and grapevines. It was made in both color and colorless glass with enamel.

There was a group of boxes with knobs and finials of flowers or nude figures. The box "Primevères" has a molded design of flowers and a flower knob. It was made in both *blanc* and *couleur*. The box "Sultane," made for cigars, has an allover line design and a knob of a nude figure sitting with folded legs and arms folded behind the head. The box was made in both *blanc* and *couleur*. Other boxes with figure knobs included "Vallauris" with a molded design of leaves and flower knob and "Amour Assis"—a charming and most desirable box. It has a figure of cupid sitting on its cover and it was made in both *blanc* and *couleur*. There were several other small boxes with molded figures on their covers.

Another group of boxes had designs of birds. Two molded birds are on the cigar box called "Saint Marc"; this box was available in color. There were two boxes with designs of molded peacocks. One box has a peacock with a large spreading tail, the other box has a design of three peacocks. Both boxes were available in colorless crystal (*blanc*). There was a box with two pigeons sitting among blossoming branches, a similar box with two birds, another box with tropical birds with long feathered tails, and a box with two swans. A rectangular cigarette box has an allover design of flying swallows, and another box has a swirling design of flying tomtits. The majority of these boxes were made in *blanc*.

Of special interest are the egg-shaped boxes. There were just two of these, one with a design of periwinkle flowers in relief and the other with a pressed design of chicks in ovals. These boxes were available in both colored and colorless crystal.

Deer and foliage decorated the panels of a box in Art Deco style called "Chantilly" and "Victoire" was another Art Deco of a winged figure with a sword. Both of these boxes were available in colorless crystal. There were many boxes with designs of flowers including roses, zinnias, dahlias, cherry blossoms, and lily of the valley. Particularly decorative are "Roses en Relief," a box with ropes of naturalistic roses, and "Panier de Roses," a box with a basket of roses that matched the flacon of the same design. These boxes were all made in colorless glass. A group of dancing nudes with garlands of flowers are especially interesting. There is also a figure of a veiled nude holding a vase from which falls a decorative stream of water, and another box with two figures wearing ballet tutus. An important box has a design of two nude sirens with pearly tresses. Attractive box designs with insects include one with three dragonflies, one with beetles and garlands of leaves, and one called "Cigales" which is divided into six triangular panels and decorated with a design of cicadas in relief.

Any boxes with designs of nudes are good collectors' items and the box with small cupids called "Amours," the box with two angels' heads, "Anges," "Victoire," and the egg-shaped boxes, are also rare boxes. These boxes were made in both *blanc* and *couleur* in large quantities and none of these original designs are now being made. The current production of Lalique boxes includes a design called "Cactus," "Dahlia," and another floral pattern, and a box with a metal mounting and a molded design of two nudes on the cover. All of these patterns except "Cactus" were first made after 1932 and possibly as late as 1950. A square box with an engraved cat's head was made c. 1950.

A group of coffrets or jewel cases were decorated with the following designs in plaques: "Monnaie du Pape" (a pattern of honesty leaves), "Papillons" (butterflies), "Chrysanthèmes," and "Figurines." These were all available in quantities of thousands in 1932.

Boxes are not inexpensive. No Lalique glass is inexpensive but if your purse does not allow you to collect large vases, boxes offer an interesting alternative; so far they are not in demand and thus not overpriced. There are over seventy different designs and they include Lalique's repertory of important designs. All boxes are signed, usually with the molded block letter mark "R.Lalique." The majority of the boxes were made in both *blanc* and *couleur*.

Boxes and Bonbonnières listed in the 1932 Lalique Catalogue include the following:

No. 1   Boîte ronde "Paon" (peacock) 450 *blanc* or clear glass.

No. 2   Boîte ronde "Coq" (cock) 300 *blanc*, 325 *couleur*.

No. 3   Boîte ronde "Amour assis" (with figure of cupid on cover) 375 *blanc*, 425 *couleur*.

No. 4   Boîte ovale "Roses en relief" 450 *blanc*. 500 *couleur*.

No. 5   Boîte ronde "Louveciennes" (two veiled dancing figures) 300 *blanc*.

No. 6   Boîte ronde "Ermenonville" (veiled dancing figure with urn) 250 *blanc*.

No. 7   Boîte ronde "Fontenay" (two dancing nudes with garlands of flowers) 165 *blanc*.

No. 9   Boîte ronde "1 Figurine et Raisins" (Nude figurine with grapes) 200 *blanc*.

No. 10   Boîte ronde "1 Figurine et Bouquets" (figurine with flowers) 200 *blanc*.

No. 11   Boîte ronde "2 Figurines et Branches" (two figurines with garlands of leaves) 200 *blanc*.

No. 14   Boîte ronde "4 Papillons" (four butterflies on cover) 100 *blanc*, 185 *couleur*.

No. 14 Boîte ronde "4 Scarabées" (four scarabs on cover) 165 *blanc*, 185 *couleur*.

No. 20 Boîte ovale "Amours" (dancing children on cover) 200 *blanc*.

No. 21 Boîte ovale "Panier de Roses" (basket of roses on cover) 200 *blanc*.

No. 22 Boîte ovale "Gabrielle" (powder puffs on cover) 200 *blanc*.

No. 23 Boîte ovale "Cygnes" (swans on cover) 200 *blanc*.

No. 24 Boîte ovale "2 Danseuses" (two dancers in ballet skirts on cover) 200 *blanc*.

No. 26 Boîte ronde "Pommier du Japan" (cherry blossoms on cover) 150 *blanc*, 175 *couleur*.

No. 28 Boîte ronde "Guirlande de Graines" (cover with design of grain) 100 *blanc*.

No. 29 Boîte ronde "Houppes" (powder puff design) 250 *couleur*.

No. 30 Boîte ronde "3 Paons" (cover with three peacocks) 125 *blanc*.

No. 31 Boîte ronde "Victoire" (cover with winged man with sword) 125 *blanc*.

No. 32 Boîte ronde "2 Figurines" (cover with two nudes and flowers) 125 *blanc*.

No. 33 Boîte ronde "1 Grand vase" (cover design of large vase with stopper of flowers) 125 *blanc*.

No. 34 Boîte ronde "2 Pigeons" (cover with design of two pigeons) 125 *blanc*.

No. 35 Boîte ronde "2 Oiseaux" (cover with two birds and flowers) 125 *blanc*.

No. 37 Boîte ronde "3 Vases" (vases and flowers) 125 *blanc*.

No. 39 Boîte ronde "Anges" (design of angel heads) 125 *blanc*.

No. 41 Boîte ronde grande "Muguets" (cover with design of lily of the valley) 425 *couleur*.

No. 42 Boîte ronde grande "Cyprins" (cover with design of goldfish) 450 *couleur*.

No. 43 Boîte ronde grande "2 Sirènes" (cover design with two dancing nudes and bubbles) 42 *couleur.*

No. 44 Boîte ronde grande "Cigales" (cover divided into six sections each with figure of cicada) 375 *couleur.*

No. 45 Boîte ronde moyenne "Georgette" (cover design of three dragonflies) 350 *couleur.*

No. 46 Boîte ronde moyenne "3 Dahlias" (large dahlias) 300 *couleur.*

No. 47 Boîte ronde moyenne "6 Dahlias" (six small dahlias) 325 *couleur.*

No. 49 Boîte ronde petite "Cléones" (cover design of insects and leaves) 175 *couleur.*

No. 50 Boîte ronde petite "Tokio" (cover of bursting blossom) 165 *couleur.*

No. 51 Boîte ronde petite "Libellules" (cover dragonfly design) 160 *couleur.*

No. 52 Boîte ronde petite "Mésanges" (cover with six tomtits with spread wings) 150 *couleur.*

No. 53 Boîte à cigarettes "Hirondelles" (rectangular box with design of swallows) 125 *blanc.*

No. 54 Boîte à cigarettes "Zinnias" (rectangular box with cover design of zinnias) 125 *blanc.*

No. 57 Boîte ronde "Geneviève" (cover design of stylized feathers and figures of two birds in center triangle) 135 *blanc.*

No. 58 Boîte ronde "Compiègne" (design of tropical birds and foliage) 95 *blanc.*

No. 59 Boîte ronde "Fontainebleau" (cover design of animals) 95 *blanc.*

No. 61 Boîte ronde "Meudon" (flowers and foliage) 95 *blanc.*

No. 62 Boîte ronde "Chantilly" (design of deer and foliage divided into six sections) 95 *blanc.*

No. 63 Boîte ronde "Cheveux de Vénus" (small box with center finial on cover) 100 *blanc.*

No. 64   Boîte ronde "Isabelle" (floral design) 70 *blanc*.

No. 65   Boîte ronde "Gui" (cover design of mistletoe) 70 *blanc*, 80 *couleur*.

No. 66   Boîte ronde "Degas" (figure in center of cover) 75 *blanc*.

No. 67   Boîte ronde "Lucie" (cover design of forget-me-nots) 65 *blanc*.

No. 68   Boîte ronde "Vaucluse" (cover design of leaves) 65 *blanc*.

No. 69   Boîte ronde "Marguerites" (allover design of marguerites) 50 *blanc*.

No. 70   Boîte ronde "Emiliane" (allover flower design) 55 *blanc*.

No. 71   Boîte ronde "Coquilles" (shell design in eight sections) 45 *blanc*, 55 *couleur*.

No. 75   Boîte ronde "Roger" (clear glass cabochons and enameled background of birds and foliage) 200 *couleur*, 200 *émaillé*.

No. 76   Boîte hexagonale "Sainte-Nectaire" (stylized swirl design of leaves) 40 *blanc*.

No. 77   Boîte ronde moyenne "Primevères" (design of flowers in relief) 200 *blanc*, 225 *couleur*.

No. 78   Boîte ovale "Dinard" (relief design of roses) 175 *blanc*.

No. 79   Boîte à cigares "Roméo" (fluted design with sliding cover) 550 *blanc*.

No. 80   Boîte à cigares "Corona" (allover design of stylized leaves) 600 *blanc*.

No. 81   Boîte ronde "Saint-Marc" (two birds in relief on cover) 450 *couleur*.

No. 82   Boîte oeuf "Pervenches" (egg-shaped box with pressed design of periwinkle flowers) 90 *blanc*, 100 *couleur*.

No. 83   Boîte carrée "Sultane" (box of allover rope design in relief and seated figure of nude with legs crossed and arms folded back head on cover of box) 350 *blanc*, 450 *couleur*.

No. 84   Boîte ronde "Vallauris" (cover design of leaves in relief and finial of berries) 150 *blanc*, 185 *couleur*.

No. 85 Boîte oeuf "Poussins" (egg-shaped box with medallions of chicks in relief) 110 *blanc*.

No. 86 Boîte ronde grande "Primevères" (box with design of flowers in relief) 275 *blanc*, 325 *couleur*.

No. 87 Boîte carrée "Palmettes" (design of palm fronds in relief) 240 *blanc*.

There were also coffrets with plaques of butterflies, chrysanthemums, figurines, and monnaie du pape leaves in relief. These small boxes were made in quantities of thousands in both *blanc* and colored glass.

"Houppes," round box with design of powder puffs. Made for Coty L'Origan powder. c.1913. (John Jesse Gallery.)

"4 Scarabées" round box with relief designs of beetles. No. 15. R. Lalique before 1912. (John Jesse Gallery.)

"Roger," round box of clear and frosted glass with designs of birds, grape vines and grapes in black enamel. No. 75. R. Lalique, before 1932. (John Jesse Gallery.)

Covered Box with relief Art Nouveau design of two draped figures. R. Lalique before 1932. (Editions Graphiques Ltd.)

Above left, "Amour Assis," round box with floral decoration and figure of cupid sitting on cover of box. No. 3. Made in c.1910. (Catalogue des Verreries de René Lalique. 1932.)

Below, Box, dark green glass with design of intertwined thistle branches; silver hinges and clasp in form of scarabs. Length, 17.8 cm.; height, 7.7 cm. Lalique c.1910-1920. (The Corning Museum of Glass.)

❧❧ LAMPS, LIGHTING FIXTURES, AND ARCHITECTURAL DETAILS

From the beginning of his career as a glassmaker Lalique made use of the effects of light and glass. He designed decorative plaques of glass with engraved designs which were illuminated by indirect lighting in their bases. Many of these plaques were later provided with shades and thus made into lamps. There is a lamp with three nude figures, another with butterflies engraved in its shaft, one of a centaur, a circular lamp engraved with a goat, and one with a design of three fish. These lamps are all marked "R.Lalique" together with the catalogue number in block letters. The shades are of glass with engraved line designs. A lamp with base and design of stylized petals called "Tears" was first made in c. 1927. There was also a lamp with figures of caryatides on the shaft and an engraved shade with lines of stylized leaves. Another lamp is upheld by two figures of nude infants at its base, and one called "Feuillage" (foliage) has a vase-shaped base ornamented with a wide band of leaves; the glass shade is engraved with a spiral leaf design. An iron-mounted glass lamp has a hemispherical shade of gray glass deep molded with an Art Deco pattern of curves. The shade is engraved on the rim in handscript "R.Lalique." These lamps were made 1925–1930. They were not included in the 1932 Catalogue but must have been in a separate catalogue of Lalique lamps.

A catalogue—"Lalique Lights and Decorations"—distributed by Breves Galleries, London, in 1928 illustrates a group of Lalique flacon-type lights with frosted vertically ribbed molded glass flacon bases and tiara-like or fan-shaped plaques engraved with decorative designs. These designs included "Cupids" (16 inches), "Apple Blossoms" (16 inches), "Pigeons" (16 inches), and "Love Birds" (17 inches). There was also a group of smaller lights including "Dandelion" (6½ inches), "Roses" (7 inches), "Carnation" (7 inches), "Almond Blossom" (7 inches), "Swallows" (7½ inches), "Cupids" (8¼ inches), and "Apple Blossom" (8 inches). These lights with engraved nosegay stoppers were similar to some Lalique flacons made for Roger et Gallet perfume. These are some of the most decorative pieces made by Lalique. Because of the delicacy of the stoppers they are hard to find in perfect condition.

Lalique also made large ceiling lights and wall fixtures. These included large crystal lusters or chandeliers of traditional shaped branches as well as modern star-shaped designs with molded leaf patterns. Lighting bowls were made in various sizes from 17 inches to 20 inches in diameter. They were made in white, smoky gray, or brown glass in contrasts of clear and frosted glass. There were also some in opalescent glass. The designs included Lalique's repertory of motifs—shells, leaves, flowers, fruit, birds, and butterflies. There was also an Art Deco design of bold curves and one called "Soleil" (sun) and a strange design of stalactites made in "ice color." A lighting bowl of the siren design was made in opaline glass. A design with borders of roses was in frosted glass with the molded design of roses in brown or white. Another bowl had an Art Deco design of curves or *rinceau*. It was available in white or amber and the same design was made in a table lamp. Many of these lighting bowls were both molded and engraved.

There were also hanging balls with allover designs such as mistletoe which was made in brown frosted glass with the berries in relief. Other hanging balls were in sunflower, dahlia, leaf, and Art Deco triangular designs. A Lalique hanging shade of hemispherical form molded in opalescent glass with raised bosses set in intaglio sunbursts, complete with hanging chains and hook, was sold at Sotheby's, Belgravia, on March 28, 1973. It had the engraved mark "R.Lalique France" and brought about £25.

Torchères and lanterns were made in traditional shapes with panels of molded glass and there were also lanterns with designs of modern spirals and squares in Art Deco style.

Wall plaques and corner lights consisted of a frosted bowl for light globes and a panel of glass engraved with designs such as tulips, dahlias, ivy leaves, beech leaves, shells, berries, and birds. The mistletoe wall light was made in frosted glass in brown with berries in relief and the dahlia corner light was available in brown, green, or white. A shell wall plaque was made in opalescent glass. According to the Breves Galleries catalogue only a certain number of each design was made and then the molds were destroyed. The pieces were marked "R.Lalique France," usually engraved. Arrangements could be made for installation. Lalique also designed complete decorations for rooms or for a complete house including glass doors, wall panels, and screens. There are Lalique lighting fixtures, doors, and screens available to collectors today and some were even installed in Park Avenue, New York, apartments.

Lalique glass relates to both fashion and furnishing and for this reason it continued in popularity with the buying public. Many of the pieces have the graceful affectations of Art Nouveau but with an order and simplicity of Art Deco. But Lalique glass has held little interest for collectors and there are those who term Lalique as glorified pressed glass. Indeed Lalique glass has been neglected by the antique collector for almost twenty years. However, now within the last few years the number of collectors of Lalique glass has increased enormously and with the present interest in Art Deco and the art and decoration of the 1920s and 1930s, especially that of France, Lalique glass has again come into its own. In addition to scores of private collectors Lalique is now collected by many museums including the Chrysler Museum at Norfolk, Virginia, The Toledo Museum of Art, The Smithsonian Institution and others both in America and abroad.

Iron-mounted glass lamp.
Hemispherical shade in grey
glass deep molded with pattern
of crescents. Shade engraved
on rim in script. "R. Lalique."
c.1925.

Light cover, body vertically ribbed
and fan-shaped crystal engraved with
prunus. Height, 16¼ inches. Lalique.
c.1925. (Christie's. Photo, A .C.
Cooper.)

Lamp, two figurines holding wreath set on bronze stand. c.1926. (Collection of Charles and Mary Magriel.)

Chandelier or lustre, Bucarest design. R. Lalique. (Breves Gallery catalogue, 1928.)

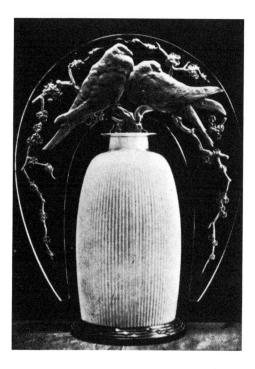

Above, left,
Lalique light. Pigeons Engraved
stopper with frosted moulded
base. (Greves Gallery catalogue,
1928.)

Above right,
Lalique light. Love Birds.
Engraved stopper with frosted
moulded base. A globe inside the
vase furnishes the light.
(Breves Gallery catalogue, 1928.)

Chandelier or lustre, Paris design.
R. Lalique. (Breves Gallery
catalogue, 1928.)

Bibliography

L'Art Verrier à l'Aube du XXe Siècle. Editions Galerie des Arts Décoratifs, S.A., Lausanne, 1973.

"Catalogue des Verreries de René Lalique." René Lalique & Cie. Paris, 1932.

"Decorative Arts 1880–1973." Sotheby & Co. Catalogue. March 9, 1970.

"Decorative Arts 1880–1939." Sotheby's Belgravia Sales Catalogue. March 8, 1972.

——————. Sotheby's Belgravia Sales Catalogue. March 28, 1973.

——————. Sotheby's Belgravia Sales Catalogue. June 22, 1973.

Geoffroy, Gustave. *René Lalique*. Paris, 1922.

Janson, Dora Jane. "From Slave to Siren." *Art News,* May, 1971.

"Lalique Lights and Decoration." Breves Galleries Catalogue. London, 1928.

"La Presse et l'Exposition des Oeuvres de René Lalique." Musée des Arts Décoratifs. Paris, 1933.

Rheims, Maurice. "L'Objet 1900." *Arts et Métiers Graphiques*. Paris, 1964.

Vever, Henri. *La Bijouterie Française au XIXe Siècle*. 3 vols. Paris, 1908.